GWINNETT COUNTY PUBLIC LIBRARY

W9-BSL-766

# World War II: Essential Histories

# World War II

## The War at Sea

Robert O'Neill, Series Editor; Philip D. Grove, Mark J. Grove, and Alastair Finlan

New York

This edition published in 2010 by:

The Rosen Publishing Group, Inc.
29 East 21st Street
New York, NY 10010

Additional end matter copyright © 2010 by The Rosen Publishing Group, Inc.

All rights reserved. No part of this publication may be reproduced, stored in a retrieval system or transmitted in any form or by any means, without the prior written consent of the publisher.

### Library of Congress Cataloging-in-Publication Data

Grove, Philip D.
World War II. The war at sea / Philip D. Grove, Mark J. Grove, and Alastair Finlan.
    p. cm.—(World War II: Essential histories)
"Robert O'Neill, series editor."
Originally published as v. 3 in The Second World War. Oxford : Osprey, 2002–2003.
Includes bibliographical references and index.
ISBN 978-1-4358-9131-9 (library binding)
1. World War, 1939–1945—Naval operations—Juvenile literature. I. Grove, Mark J. II. Finlan, Alastair. III. O'Neill, Robert John. IV. Second World War. V. Title. VI. Title: World War Two.
D770.G767 2010
940.54'293—dc22
2009031237

*Manufactured in Malaysia*

CPSIA Compliance Information: Batch #TW10YA: For Further Information contact Rosen Publishing, New York, New York at 1-800-237-9932

Copyright © 2002 Osprey Publishing Limited. First published in paperback by Osprey Publishing Limited.

**On the cover:** Detail from battle of Cape Matapan *(Imperial War Museum)*

# Contents

# Introduction

World War II at sea was a more genuinely global conflict than either the war on land or that in the air. Most of the world's navies were involved and the conflict raged across every ocean and major sea. The struggles in the Atlantic, Mediterranean, Indian, and Pacific oceans were complemented by lesser-known battles in the Arctic, Baltic, Black, and Red seas. Although the latter were geographically smaller and more confined, they were of no less interest and significance, for each aided in the overall aim of the combatants: supremacy on the land.

The sheer scale of the conflict can never be underestimated. The war was immense, not only in terms of geography, but also in terms of naval strengths, manpower, and industrial output. Far more than any before, this was a war not just of naval skill and tactics, but of economics and technology. Yet most navies found themselves unprepared for war and were forced to develop and expand at a frightening rate, some more successfully than others. Some, such as the Royal Canadian Navy and the Soviet Navy, expanded from next to nothing to become huge fighting forces by the end of the conflict, while the established navies, particularly the American and British, grew to unprecedented proportions, with millions of personnel in naval uniforms and thousands of vessels to control.

Navies found themselves forced to make unexpected changes to their preconceived strategies. Technology, numbers, and naval platforms all underwent a revolution. The battleship was, for most navies in the 1920s and 1930s, the centerpiece of naval thinking. It was replaced by the submarine and the aircraft carrier at the heart of fleet tactics. The submarines' stealth and the carriers' firepower and range undermined the romance of the floating fortresses. There were still those who held onto the image of the great gray battleships dueling each other to the death, and they were not to be disappointed. But these were the dying moments of past technical glories. World War II belonged to a new and different naval age.

Yet navies did have to remember one role from the days before the steel battleship. Initially shunned by most in the interwar period, amphibious operations grew in significance as the war progressed, to the point of even deciding the war in western Europe, the Mediterranean, and the Pacific. Without the huge Allied amphibious capability, millions would have remained enslaved by Axis occupation.

The war was not all about sailors and ships and soldiers storming the beaches. This was also a war of the civilian, of industry, and of supply. With 70 percent of the world's surface covered in water and all of the warring countries dependent on materials from overseas, it was only natural that the seas would be a vital supply route and thus the war's biggest battleground. Caught up in this were the various merchant navies and their seamen. Civilian mariners now wore two caps. They were legitimate targets as never before for the enemy, but they were also heroes for a country's survival. They struggled and suffered at the hands of mines, torpedoes, gunfire, and bombs, with loss rates higher than most naval forces during the war. Three merchant campaigns in particular proved vital: the Battle of the Atlantic for the Allied convoys; the Mediterranean for the British submarines; and the Pacific for the American submariners. Success in these campaigns enabled victory on land.

The enormity and brutality of the struggle have helped it remain fresh in the minds of many, and not just those who lived through the conflict. History is remembered and punctuated by the great periods of war, not peace, which may help to explain the interest in the naval side of World War II. The ability to explore long-lost ships deep in the oceans of the world and the eagerness to display as many artifacts from the war as possible, provide further reasons for our collective interest in the war; nor, of course, should it be forgotten that the Allied victory in this struggle shaped the world in which we live today.

This book seeks to add to understanding by introducing those with an interest in the subject to a fresh review of the events, technologies, and personalities involved in the war. This will be done by illustrating the events and course of the war in the Atlantic and Indian oceans and the Mediterranean Sea. We will also highlight the better-known aspects and personalities of the war in these theaters, while inviting the reader to ponder some less familiar areas.

# Chronology

**1921** **November–February**
1922 Washington Naval Treaty: naval
arms race is halted

**1922** **February** Anglo-Japanese Naval
Alliance ends

**1930** **April 22** London Naval Treaty
restricts warships further

**1934** **December 19** Japan refuses to be
bound by Washington Naval Treaties

**1935** **April** United States Neutrality Act
**June 18** Anglo-German Naval Pact

**1936** **January 15** Japan leaves London
Naval Conference
**March 25** Great Britain, United
States, and France sign London
Naval Treaty

**1937** **July 7** Sino-Japanese War begins
**December** Nanking falls to
Japanese forces
**December 12** USS *Panay* sunk by
Japanese aircraft

**1938** **September** Munich crisis.
Czechoslovakian Sudetenland
handed over to Germany

**1939** **Spring** Remainder of Czechoslovakia
occupied.
**Summer** Great Britain and France
issue guarantees to Poland
**August** U-boats and "Pocket
Battleships" deploy to the Atlantic
**August 23–24** Nazi–Soviet
Non-Aggression Pact signed
**August 31** Royal Navy of Great
Britain mobilizes for war
**September 1** Germany attacks
Poland

**September 3** British Prime Minister
Chamberlain forms War Cabinet with
Churchill as First Lord of the
Admiralty; Great Britain and France
declare war against Germany;
SS *Athenia* is torpedoed off the
northwest coast of Ireland by *U-30*
(112 dead, including 28 Americans)
**September 4** Royal Air Force (RAF)
begins anti-German shipping strikes
**September 7** Convoys initiated
**September 14** *U-39* sunk by Royal
Navy destroyers – the first German loss
**September 17** HMS *Courageous* sunk
by *U-29* while on anti-submarine patrol
**September 26** A Dornier 18 flying
boat is shot down by HMS *Ark Royal's*
Skuas – the first Luftwaffe (German air
force) aircraft to be destroyed by Britain
**October 14** HMS *Royal Oak* sunk by
*U-47* while at anchor in Scapa Flow
**November 3** US Congress passes the
"Cash and Carry" amendment to the
US Neutrality Act enabling Britain to
purchase military goods from the US
**December 13** "Battle of the River
Plate"
**December 17** *Graf Spee* scuttled by
her captain outside Montevideo harbor

**1940** **February** Great Britain breaks
German Enigma Code
**February 16** HMS *Cossack* captures
the German supply ship *Altmark* in
Norwegian waters
**March 1** Hitler issues final directive
concerning invasion of Norway
**March 31** *Atlantis*, the first of the
German armed merchantmen
raiders, sails
**April 7** Allied forces prepare to
invade Norway
**April 9** German forces invade
Denmark and Norway

**April 10–13** Two battles of Narvik

**April 14** British forces land in Norway

**May 10** France and the Low Countries invaded by Germany; British forces seize Iceland

**May 16** Mediterranean closed by Admiralty to normal merchant traffic; 20,000 miles (32,200 kilometers) added to convoy routes

**May 26–June 4** Operation Dynamo: the withdrawal of Allied troops from Dunkirk

**June 4–9** Allies evacuate Norway

**June 8** HMS *Glorious* and escorting destroyers sunk by German battlecruisers *Gneisenau* and *Scharnhorst*

**June 10** Italy declares war; Italian air attacks begin on Malta

**June 13** A new $1.3 billion Navy Bill is signed by Roosevelt

**June 15** Another Navy Bill provides for 10,000 new aircraft and 16,000 new aircrew for the expanding US naval air service

**June 22** France signs armistice with Germany

**June 30** German forces begin to occupy the Channel Islands

**July 3–5** Gibraltar-based Force H successfully neutralizes French naval force at Mers-el-Kebir; further attacks were made here and at other French-held ports

**July 19** "Two-Ocean Navy Expansion Act" is signed by Roosevelt, adding an additional 1,325,000 tons of warships and 15,000 planes to the US Navy

**August 1** Hitler issues Directive 17 for the invasion of Britain

**August 2** Operation Hurry; first Royal Navy "ferry flight" of aircraft to Malta from HMS *Argus*, the first of some 719 aircraft flown from aircraft carriers successfully reaching Malta

**August 16–19** British personnel are evacuated by the Royal Navy from Berbera, British Somaliland, following invasion by Italian forces

**August 16** First British sinking of a U-boat, *U-51*, by air-dropped depth charge

**August 17** Hitler announces a total blockade of the British Isles

**August 27** RAF Coastal Command establishes a convoy protection base in Iceland

**September** Britain strengthens Home Fleet in preparation for invasion

**September 3** British–United States lend-lease agreement for 50 US "Four Stacker" destroyers in return for use of British bases

**September 9** New US government bill for 210 vessels worth $5,500,000,000

**September 20–22** Convoy HX-72 loses 12 ships to U-boat attack

**September 22** Japan enters Indochina

**September 23–26** French fleet in Dakar attacked by Royal Navy and Free French forces

**October 12** Hitler postpones Operation Sea Lion

**October 17–19** Convoy SC-7 loses 21 ships out of 30

**October 19–20** Convoy HX-79 loses 12 ships out of 49; consequently, there is an increase in escort numbers

**November 5** Armed merchant cruiser *Jervis Bay* defends 32 merchant ships in convoy HX-84 from the *Admiral Scheer*; *Jervis Bay* and five other merchantmen are lost

**November 11–12** Operation Judgement; 21 Swordfish from HMS *Illustrious* strike the Italian fleet in the harbor of Taranto; half of the Italian battle fleet is disabled

**November 18–19** Air-to-surface vessel (ASV) radar on board an RAF Sunderland achieves first operational detection

**1941** **January 2** The Liberty ship, a mass-produced standardized merchant ship design, is announced

**February 12** Heavy cruiser *Hipper* sinks seven ships from 19-strong convoy SLS-64

**March** First B-24 Liberators enter RAF service

**March 6** Churchill issues his Battle of the Atlantic Directive

**March 12** Roosevelt presents Congress with his Lend-Lease Bill

**March 28** Battle of Matapan; Admiral Cunningham's aircraft carrier and battleships sink three Italian heavy cruisers and damage battleship *Veneto Vittorio*

**April 6** Royal Navy lands 6,000 troops in Greece

**April 22–May 5** Royal Navy evacuates British forces from Greece

**May 18** *Bismarck* and *Prinz Eugen* sail for the Atlantic

**May 20** German forces attack Crete

**May 24** HMS *Hood* sunk in action with *Bismarck* and *Prinz Eugen*

**May 27** *Bismarck* sunk

**May 27–June 1** Royal Navy begins Allied withdrawal from Crete and sustains heavy casualties

**June** HMS *Audacity* commissioned – the first escort carrier (CVE), converted from a German merchantman

**June 12** Royal Navy lands Anglo-Indian force in the port of Assab, Italian East Africa

**August 12** Roosevelt and Churchill sign the Atlantic Charter on board HMS *Prince of Wales*

**October 31** US destroyer *Reuben James* is sunk with the loss of 100 sailors by a U-boat while escorting convoy HX-156 – the first US ship lost

**November 1** First action involving a Catapult Armed Merchantman (CAM)

**November 14** HMS *Ark Royal* sinks in sight of Gibraltar from a single torpedo fired by *U-81*

**November 25** The battleship HMS *Barham* is sunk in the Mediterranean by *U-331*

**December 7** Imperial Japan attacks Pearl Harbor and southeast Asia

**December 10** HMS *Prince of Wales* and *Repulse* sunk by Indochina-based Japanese Navy aircraft

**December 19** Italian frogmen using "human torpedoes" damage battleships HMS *Queen Elizabeth* and *Valiant* in Alexandria

**December 21** HMS *Audacity* sunk by *U-751*; Swordfish equipped with ASV sinks U-boat in darkness

**1942** **February 11–13** German Operation Cerberus – the "Channel Dash"; *Scharnhorst*, *Gneisenau* and *Prinz Eugen* successfully return to Germany from Brest through the English Channel

**February** Admiral Somerville's Eastern Fleet begins arrival in Indian Ocean

**March 9** Albacores from HMS *Victorious* carry out an unsuccessful strike against the *Tirpitz* in open seas

**April 2–8** Japanese carrier aircraft attack Ceylon

**April 9** HMS *Hermes* sunk by Japanese carrier aircraft

**May 5** Operation Ironclad; British forces invade Vichy-held Madagascar

**August 4** HMS *Eagle* is sunk by *U-73* as part of Malta convoy Operation Pedestal

**August 19** British and Canadian forces sustain heavy casualties during raid on Dieppe

**November 6** Vichy French forces surrender in Madagascar

**November 8** Operation Torch; Anglo-American invasion of Vichy French North Africa; by November 11, French resistance has ceased

**November 15** HMS *Avenger*, a CVE, blows up west of Gibraltar following a torpedo hit from *U-155*

**1943** **January 30** Admiral Dönitz replaces Admiral Raeder as head of the Kriegsmarine (German navy)

**April 28–May 6** Convoy ONS-2 fights off 51 U-boats, sinking seven

**May 12** Surrender of Axis forces in North Africa

**May 22** Dönitz temporarily withdraws U-boats from action against convoys
**July 10** Operation Husky; Allied invasion of Sicily
**August 27** HMS *Egret* sunk in the Bay of Biscay by German air-launched, rocket- propelled, anti-ship missile, the Hs 293
**September 3** Allies land in Italy
**September 9** Operation Avalanche; Allied invasion of Salerno
**September 11** Italian fleet surrenders in Malta; Italian battleship *Roma* sunk en route by two German air-launched Fritz X glide bombs (September 9)
**September 21** Royal Navy midget submarines attack the *Tirpitz* in Norwegian fjord
**December 26** *Scharnhorst* sunk off North Cape by British force led by battleship HMS *Duke of York*

1944 **January 22** Allies land at Anzio
**April 3** Aircraft from HMS *Furious* and *Victorious* and four CVEs attack the *Tirpitz* in Norwegian fjord – damaged but not sunk; a further attack

in July is disrupted by a dense smoke screen
**June 6** D-Day; Operation Neptune, the naval component of Overlord, the invasion of Normandy is launched
**August 15** Operation Dragoon; Allied invasion of southern France
**August 24** Aircraft from HMS *Furious* and *Indefatigable* and two CVEs attack the *Tirpitz* – again it is damaged but not sunk
**November 12** RAF Lancasters armed with 12,000 lb (5,450 kg) "Tallboy" bombs sink the *Tirpitz*

1945 **April 30** Death of Hitler – Dönitz becomes new head of state
**May 7** SS *Sneland* and SS *Avondale Park* are the last ships sunk by German U-boat, *U-2336*, in World War II; *U-320* was the last U-boat sunk in the war (by British aircraft); Germany surrenders
**August 6 and 9** Atomic weapons dropped on Hiroshima and Nagasaki
**September 2** Japanese surrender signed aboard USS *Missouri* in Tokyo Bay

# World War II

World War II was the most violent, all-encompassing conflict in human history, yet as wars go, it started slowly. Europe was, once again, the source of the war, which inexorably spread to Africa, the Americas, Asia, and their surrounding oceans. The clash of competing ideologies – between liberal democracies and militaristic fascist states – eventually dragged the Communist Soviet Union into the fight as well. For several politicians in 1939, with the bitter memory of the Great War of 1914–18 still fresh in their minds, the clarion of war was all too familiar. It was a highly reluctant Britain under the direction of Prime Minister Neville Chamberlain that declared war on Germany on September 3, 1939, after Adolf Hitler had ordered his armed forces into Poland just two days earlier.

The origins of World War II can be traced back to the embers of World War I, when an exhausted Germany agreed to an armistice with the Allies (Britain, France, United States, Japan, and Italy) out of which emerged the controversial Treaty of Versailles, signed in 1919. A common sentiment among bitter German soldiers, including a young Austrian-born corporal named Adolf Hitler, held that the German army had been stabbed in the back by weak civilians in the fatherland, whose negotiations for peace had robbed it of the victory that was just around the corner. The reality was quite different: Germany was economically exhausted after four long years of fighting on several fronts.

The fault lay with the nature of warfare in the twentieth century, particularly the advanced technology of the machine age. World War I heralded a new type of warfare that stunned soldiers and politicians on all sides by its intensity, duration, and cost. Battles lasted weeks and months, instead of days as

the Battle of Waterloo had in 1815, and incurred tens of thousands of casualties. The first day of the Battle of the Somme in July 1916 cost the British army 60,000 casualties, of which 20,000 were fatalities. Chivalry, honor, maneuver, and young men (in millions) died in the staccato stutter of machine-gun fire, barbed wire, and trenches, while generals on all sides struggled to solve the strategic conundrum of the static battlefield.

At sea, British and German naval officers possessed the greatest accumulation of naval firepower in history, yet the test of war proved it to be indecisive and disappointing. The hallmark of naval power by 1914 was the battleship, and the rival fleets finally met at the Battle of Jutland on May 31, 1916, the outcome of which is still hotly debated today. The statistics were impressive: 28 British battleships and nine battlecruisers with a host of supporting destroyers under Admiral Sir John Jellicoe fought 16 German battleships, five battlecruisers, and smaller escorts commanded by Admiral Reinhard Scheer. On paper, it was a tactical victory for the Germans, who sank 111,980 tons of British ships and inflicted 6,945 casualties in return for a British tally of 62,233 tons sunk and 2,921 German casualties. Strategically, however, the Royal Navy emerged triumphant, for the balance of power remained firmly on the side of the British, whose numerically superior fleet (unlike the High Seas Fleet) was ready for operations the following day. Yet, glory was absent from this battle, replaced by a controversy about the failings of the Royal Navy that has raged to the present day.

Did Britannia still rule the waves? This was a question reinforced by a new threat after 1916 – the submarine or the U-boat – which nearly strangled Britain through sinking merchant ships, the vital supply

## Europe steers toward war

1. The Maginot Line was a series of fortifications designed as a physical barrier between France and Germany.
2. Hitler remilitarizes the Rhineland, March 1936.
3. Austria annexed by Germany, March 1938.
4. Germany acquires significant portions of Czechoslovakia as a result of the infamous Munich Agreement.
5. Germany invades Poland in early September 1939.
6. The Soviet Union annexes parts of Eastern Europe as a result of the 1939 Nazi–Soviet Non-Aggression Pact.
7. Germany's brilliant military campaign through the Ardennes forest led to the fall of France in 1940.
8. On June 22, 1941, Hitler launched Operation Barbarossa, the invasion of the Soviet Union.

German expansion

Soviet expansion

links of the nation. In April 1917 alone, the height of German unrestricted submarine warfare, total sinkings amounted to approximately 900,000 tons, a figure that simply could not be sustained in the short term. In terms of oulook and equipment the Royal Navy was ill-equipped to meet this threat. For hundreds of years, the surface fleet and the decisive battle had been at the core of Royal Navy operations, but now it faced an adversary against which these two elements appeared unsuitable. Submarines were not designed to be involved in fleet actions (they were very vulnerable on the surface and had limited endurance) and tended to hunt through the vast oceans as single units.

The other vexing question was how to find such an elusive foe. Unsurprisingly, considering its aggressive ethos and desire to seek the enemy, the Royal Navy adopted the wrong solution. Its hunting packs of destroyers patrolled apparently empty oceans with little success, while merchant ships were sunk in vast numbers. Desperation forced British politicians in May 1917 to order the Royal Navy to adopt the logical yet ostensibly inglorious convoy system, which rectified the rapidly declining strategic situation at sea. Shackled to the pace of the slowest ship, naval escorts at last encountered enemy submarines (drawn naturally to the merchant vessels) and by the use of gunfire, depth charges,

The standard battleship of World War I mirrored the revolutionary HMS *Dreadnought*, produced by the Royal Navy in 1906. This ship revolutionized naval warfare by its size (18,000 tons), speed (21 knots) and firepower (10 12-inch guns), which rendered all other ships of this category obsolete and triggered a naval construction race between Britain and Germany. (Naval Historical Foundation, NH 63367)

and hydrophones finally controlled the threat to merchant ships.

The war ended with the armistice signed on November 11, 1918. The terms of the armistice marked the demise of the German High Seas Fleet of nine battleships, five battlecruisers, and over 50 supporting warships, which was subsequently interned under the control of the Royal Navy at Scapa Flow. The following year, on June 21, 1919, this fleet scuttled itself – a last gesture of a once powerful force.

The Allies, joined by the United States in the final year of the war, now counted the cost of four years of warfare that had been conducted on an unprecedented scale. The expenditure had enormous consequences for nations and their navies in the interwar period. Countries and economies in Europe lay in ruins, debt accumulated, and the postwar global recession grew remorselessly,

reaching a peak with the Wall Street crash of 1929. Britain faced huge financial problems in the 1920s and 1930s, compounded by the global commitments of empire, and these called for stringent budgeting as well as cutbacks in standing armed forces.

For the Royal Navy, the golden age of ship construction was over and it faced a variety of new challenges with ever-diminishing resources. One of the great technological leaps of the Great War emerged in the form of maritime aircraft, which would dominate World War II at sea. The Royal Navy launched the first air strike from the sea on German facilities at Cuxhaven on December 25, 1914. The aircraft (but not the fledgling aircraft carriers) of the Royal Naval Air Service were amalgamated into the new Royal Air Force in April 1918 and allowed to stagnate in the shadow of the "bomber" ethos of this new service.

The British government responded to mounting financial pressures with severe cutbacks in defense spending, such as the Geddes axe in 1921, the 10-year rule (no major war was anticipated for at least 10 years in the 1920s) and arms treaties to limit naval construction, of which one of

the most significant was the Washington Naval Agreement of 1921–22. These agreements and cutbacks led to an inevitable and dramatic decline in the strength of the Royal Navy, but for the British government they represented a welcome respite from high defense spending.

Germany's position after the armistice and the subsequent signing of the Treaty of Versailles on June 28, 1919, was little short of disastrous. Despite the fact that Germany had been exhausted financially by the war, the Allies – particularly the French, who were swamped by debt – imposed crippling reparations and occupied valuable parts of Germany, such as the Rhineland and the Ruhr. Social unrest, fanned by the flames of revolution in 1918 and by economic recession, characterized the German state in the 1920s. Out of this general discontent emerged Hitler and the National Socialist (Nazi) Party.

The watchword of the new regime was economic autarky or self-sufficiency, derived from enviously noting how nations like Britain and France supported themselves through overseas colonies. German self-sufficiency was to be achieved through enhanced militarism within the state and aggressive expansionism to obtain *Lebensraum* (or living space) for the German people in Europe. For the German armed forces, this was a time of modernization and enhanced spending, with emphasis placed on the German army (Wehrmacht) and the German air force (Luftwaffe). The German navy (Kriegsmarine) enjoyed the benefits of starting anew, without the hindrance of

ABOVE For the Royal Navy, the German submarine or U-boat represented an asymmetric threat, one that its force structure – battleships and battlecruisers – seemed ill-prepared to neutralize.

RIGHT Hitler's accession to power in January 1933 marked a turning point in German foreign policy, especially relations with other foreign powers. (IWM HU 63418)

existing force structures. It embarked on a major capital ship program (breaking treaty limits with the 52,000-ton battleship *Bismarck*) as well as significant U-boat construction.

The neighboring powers of Europe watched German rearmament in the 1930s with mixed emotions. In Italy, Hitler found an ideological ally in Benito Mussolini, who shared Hitler's right-wing views and desire for expansion, reflected in the Italian invasion of Abyssinia in 1935. At sea, Italy possessed a formidable navy that by 1940 would swell to six battleships, 19 cruisers of various sizes, 61 destroyers and 105 submarines, making it a highly useful asset for German strategic plans in the Mediterranean.

*The Washington Naval Agreement*
The Washington Conference between Britain, the United States, and Japan limited these nations to a capital ship ratio of 5:5:3 (500,000 tons being the maximum for Britain) as well as the size of individual battleships to 35,000 tons. Subsequent treaties would include France and Italy, with smaller ratios.

France watched the revitalization of Germany's armed forces with great trepidation, and successive French administrations tried to use the League of Nations (founded in 1920), treaties, and finally France's armed forces to contain this longstanding threat. Though France possessed a significant navy that contained five battleships and battlecruisers, one aircraft carrier, and 15 cruisers with a host of supporting escorts, the state placed greater weight on the Maginot Line, a line of fortifications between the two countries started in 1929. Sadly, it proved to be strategic folly as the German army bypassed it in 1940 by invading Belgium.

To the east, the Soviet Union was heavily involved in its internal affairs, and its leader, Joseph Stalin, while recognizing the potential threat of Germany, focused on enemies closer to home. In 1937, he purged the Red Army of 36,671 officers, many of whom were executed; these constituted some of the finest military minds in the country. To a large extent, Stalin enjoyed the luxury of geography, having Poland as an unwilling buffer state, and he was content to contain the German threat through treaties such as the Nazi–Soviet Non-Aggression Pact of 1939.

In the Far East, Japanese expansionism into Manchuria in 1931, encouraged by militarism, exposed the weakness of the League of Nations. The lack of standing armed forces and the unwillingness of European nations to go to war over a country in Asia meant that the League could offer only moral condemnation of this overt aggression. Such inaction undoubtedly offered considerable encouragement to would-be expansionists like Hitler and Mussolini. Japan also flouted the treaty obligations concerning warship size in the 1930s and secretly built the world's biggest battleship, the 70,000-ton *Yamato* with 18.1-inch (460 mm) guns.

The only possible counterweight to this threat to European interests in the Far East, the United States, refused to join the League in 1920 and was tightly focused on returning to isolationism after the bitter experience of the First World War. Under President Roosevelt, America was wracked with financial problems in the aftermath of a global recession that left thousands of people near to starvation in poorer states such as Oklahoma. Roosevelt realized the mounting danger in Europe, but domestic pressures to remain in isolation tied his hands. Nevertheless, the US Navy underwent a significant buildup in terms of capital ships from 1933 onward, a period in which the famous Iowa class of battleships was designed.

Europe's slide into open warfare was characterized by a series of intense crises in the years leading up to 1939, the resolution of which seemed to offer the faint glimmer of hope that hostilities could be averted. To many politicians, particularly British, Hitler's attempts to overturn the harsh conditions of the Treaty of Versailles (through assertive action such as the remilitarization of the Rhineland in 1936) did not appear unreasonable. Indeed, a level of sympathy was reflected in the now vilified policy of appeasement, which is inextricably tied to the Munich Agreement of 1938, allowing Germany to annex parts of Czechoslovakia. When Britain's Prime Minister, Neville Chamberlain, returned to the nation with the signed document, he famously declared "peace in our time."

The Munich Agreement has become a powerful symbol of appeasement in international relations. Britain and France hoped that it would be the final concession, but in fact it merely encouraged Hitler to seek more. It was a rational policy that foundered on the rocks of Hitler's irrational dreams of world domination. Ironically, Britain's declaration of war was an unpleasant surprise for the German armed forces, whose rearmament program was designed for war not in 1939, but rather in the early to mid-1940s. The German navy's "Z-Plan" of 1938 was testimony to this fact, and the anticipated four aircraft carriers, 13 battleships, and 250 U-boats were little more than sketches on a design table.

Neither side was truly prepared for World War II, but for Britain and France, the odds of winning a war were better now than they would be when Germany was fully mobilized for war.

Chamberlain's claim was warmly welcomed by the average person in the street. The sound of machine-gun fire still echoed in many households in Britain; few were untouched by the mud of Flanders and the Somme. (IWM HU 4255)

# Reluctant adversaries

Britain's Royal Navy ended the First World War triumphant. It had swept the seas of the German navy and successfully blockaded Germany and its allies, so making a major contribution to their economic dislocation and ultimately to their military collapse. It had achieved, if not another Trafalgar, then certainly a strategic victory over the High Seas Fleet at Jutland in 1916 sufficient to maintain control of the seas. The manpower of both the Old and New Worlds had been brought across oceans controlled by the most powerful fleet the world had yet seen, for the Royal Navy had managed, albeit with some difficulty, to defeat the menace of a new weapons system, the submarine. Moreover, it had pioneered another, aircraft at sea, in the development and use of which by 1918 the Royal Navy undoubtedly led the world.

Nevertheless, such past achievements were not an altogether accurate pointer to the future. Britain, like the rest of the European belligerents, was economically exhausted. During the 1920s and early 1930s its navy had to struggle under increasing budget cuts. The peacetime naval estimate, for example, fell by a third. The British government seized upon the offer of parity with the United States in the Washington Naval Treaty of 1922, which restricted the size of the world's principal fleets and their main weapons, the battleship and aircraft carrier. This and later naval arms agreements, while serving to limit potential threats in the short term, would in the long run have a detrimental effect on the design and capabilities of British ships.

Although development in this period was hindered by the shortage of resources, the professionalism and quality of senior British officers would be major assets in the forthcoming campaigns, since they were of an age to have gained useful combat experience

in World War I, often in command of destroyers. The Royal Navy assiduously set about learning from its failure to destroy the weaker German fleet at Jutland. But other areas increasingly lost out. Trade defense, for example, despite the damage wrought by German U-boats in 1917 and the utter dependence of Britain on trade to prosper and imports to exist, was given a low priority, as were offensive submarine operations and, to an even greater extent, amphibious warfare.

The navy also suffered greatly from a government decision to remove its responsibility for naval aviation and, in 1918, to give it to the Royal Air Force. The world's first independent air force was eager to carve out its own niche and was little interested in operations in support of the senior service. Consequently, the aircraft that the Royal Navy was forced to operate aboard its carriers increasingly suffered in comparison to those specialist machines being ordered by the dedicated naval air services of the Americans and Japanese.

By the middle of the 1930s, British defense planners were worried about the challenges – in reality, the insoluble strategic dilemma – of an increasingly dangerous international situation. Britain was no longer in a position to protect its scattered, worldwide empire. In the Far East, imperial possessions were threatened by the rise of an aggressive and acquisitive Japan. A great naval base had been built at Singapore, which relied on the British fleet being sent from home waters to equip it. However, it became ever more apparent that this fleet would be required in European waters, where Britain's position was threatened by growing tensions with Mussolini's Fascist Italy, sitting astride the vital Mediterranean sea route, and after 1933 by the rearmament of Germany under Adolf Hitler.

While it had achieved a strategic victory over the German fleet at Jutland in 1916, the Royal Navy spent the interwar period studying the reasons why it had failed to destroy it, using exercises such as this, involving Royal Sovereign-class battleships. (IWM SP 1501)

A re-equipment program was begun. A new class of battleships – the 42,000-ton King George V class with 10 14-inch (356 millimeter) guns – was ordered. A large carrier-building program was belatedly begun, with the Illustrious class, complete with armored hangars, being ordered to supplement the original and somewhat unsatisfactory World War I–vintage conversions; *Illustrious* herself appeared in 1939. A crash building program of anti-submarine escorts, including the stalwart of the forthcoming Battle of the Atlantic, the

Flower class, was also begun. However, this expansion program was hindered by the shrinkage of the country's military industrial base. Indeed, the shortage of adequate shipbuilding and repair capacity continued to impose restrictions on Britain throughout World War II, a deficiency that could only in the end be filled by the prodigious efforts of shipyards in the United States.

After years of wrangling, responsibility for seagoing naval aviation was returned to the Royal Navy in 1937. However, naval aviation had been severely hamstrung by years of neglect: it had too many small carriers, equipped with too few, obsolete aircraft, and a significant number of officers were ignorant of both the utility and dangers of air power. The navy to which Winston Churchill was reappointed as First Lord of

Based on a civilian whale-catcher design, the Flower-class Corvette was really too slow and small for North Atlantic anti-submarine operations, and, described as able to "roll on wet grass," was certainly uncomfortable for its crew of 120. Nevertheless, it was robust and available in reasonable numbers, and it formed the backbone of the Anglo-Canadian escort force throughout the war. (IWM A4594)

the Admiralty – its political head – in September 1939 was thus in many respects ill-prepared for the coming test.

Nevertheless, Britain's main European opponent was in a far worse state of preparation. The Versailles Treaty of 1919, which had ended World War I, had severely restricted Germany's armed forces. Its navy was limited to six pre-World War I, pre-*Dreadnought*-type battleships, six light cruisers, a dozen destroyers, and a similar number of torpedo boats. It was forbidden submarines and aircraft. Admiral Erich Raeder became head of the German navy in October 1928 and remained so until January 1943, becoming Grand Admiral in April 1939. Raeder from the start argued that war with Britain had to be avoided: despite the reductions of the 1920s, British naval strength and geographical position would spell maritime disaster for Germany. Raeder, instead, concentrated on countering any potential French and Polish threats. The first postwar class of heavy units, the three Panzerschiffe, the "pocket battleships" – in effect, a somewhat flawed heavy cruiser – was designed with the French in mind.

With the coming to power of Adolf Hitler in 1933, a massive rearmament program was initiated. The first result for the navy was the construction of a new class of 11-inch (279 mm) gunned battlecruisers, of which two, *Scharnhorst* and *Gneisenau*, were eventually built out of the planned five. Raeder was forced to rely on the strategy of attacking a potential enemy's merchant navy, as Germany simply would not have the strength to take on a first-class opponent's main fleet. He favored the construction of heavy surface raiders to accomplish this, and in 1936 two battleships, *Bismarck* and *Tirpitz*, were laid down. These were immensely powerful ships, displacing 42,000 tons, well armored, with eight 15-inch (381 mm) guns and capable of almost 30 knots.

In the 1930s, the Kriegsmarine recognized the requirement to build up its own air arm, but was blocked by the head of the Luftwaffe, Herman Göring, who believed that "everything that flies belongs to me." Work was begun in 1936 on the first of a small class of aircraft carriers, the 23,000-ton *Graf Zeppelin*, which was intended to carry a powerful air group of 28 Ju-87D dive-bombers and 12 Me-109G fighters. However, construction of the *Graf Zeppelin* was suspended in May 1940 when she was 85 percent complete, and her sister ship was broken up on the stocks in the same year.

After Hitler and Raeder, the other dominating figure in the German navy was Karl Dönitz, who in 1935 became head of the newly created submarine arm of the now renamed Kriegsmarine. His efforts to persuade Hitler to develop a submarine force of around 300 did not succeed. Instead the Kriegsmarine entered the war with some 24 ocean-going boats. However, throughout the 1920s and 1930s, initially using motor torpedo boats, the submarine arm had begun to develop new tactics – such as the Wolf Pack – which were aimed at overcoming enemy merchant convoys, and which had been used to such effect during World War I.

When in 1938, to the Kriegsmarine's surprise, Hitler made it clear that it was unlikely that Germany could avoid war with Britain in the long run, a large fleet-building program, the Z-Plan, was begun. Predicated on the assumption that war would not come until 1944, the plan still had at its heart the destruction of the enemy's merchant marine. However, it called for the construction of a fleet of extremely powerful battleships, including six 56,000-ton leviathans, able to fight their way through a British-dominated North Sea and out into the hunting grounds of the Atlantic. In the meantime, with the Kriegsmarine at a considerable numerical disadvantage, Raeder continued to urge that

war with Great Britain be avoided – warnings that Hitler, almost to the eve of his invasion of Poland, appeared to accept, at least in his conversations with his naval chief.

As tension rose in Europe, France too began to re-equip its fleet, first to counter any potential Italian threat in the Mediterranean and then increasingly as a result of developments in Germany. For example, the very capable *Dunkerque* and *Strasbourg*, 26,500-ton battleships, capable of 30 knots and with eight 13-inch (330 mm) guns, were intended to counter the German Panzerschiffe pocket battleships. In the five years before the outbreak of World War II the French naval reconstruction program absorbed 27 percent of the military budget, and the French fleet under Admiral Darlan became the fourth largest in the world, its

Adolf Hitler with Admiral Dr Erich Raeder (pictured extreme right), head of the German navy from 1928 until January 1943. Hitler had a limited grasp of naval affairs. As Hitler himself admitted, "on land he was a hero, on sea a coward." He always wanted his navy to succeed in battle, but not to suffer any losses. Such a contradictory approach had a stifling effect on his admirals and commanding officers. (AKG London)

Admiral Karl Dönitz, head of the German U-boat arm throughout the Second World War and Commander-in-Chief of the navy from January 1943 and in May 1945, the Third Reich's second and last führer. (IWM HU 3652)

high-quality ships manned by long-service professionals.

The expansion of French naval power in turn influenced Italian naval developments. Like Admiral Raeder, the head of the Italian navy, Admiral Cavagnari, viewed the prospect of war with Britain as unthinkable during the 1930s. Instead, attention was exclusively given to countering the French, and it was to this end that the Italian fleet was constructed. While the Italian fleet was probably better trained than the country's other services, its ships lacked some key modern equipment, such as anti-submarine sound detection sets and radar, and naval aviation was in the hands of the Italian air force.

Across the Atlantic, since the Washington Naval Treaty, the attention of the US Navy had increasingly been drawn to the Pacific and the potential of war with Japan. It was here that the bulk of America's fleet assets, including 15 capital ships and five carriers, were deployed. Increasingly, however, after September 1939 its small Atlantic Squadron would have to deal with President Roosevelt's decision to implement a Neutrality Patrol in a bid to discourage warlike activities in the waters of the Americas. To its north, the Canadian Navy, which would end the war with no fewer than 365 ships, consisted of fewer than 2,000 men.

| The fleets of the major naval powers, January 1939 | | | | | | |
|---|---|---|---|---|---|---|
| | Britain and British Commonwealth | Germany | France | Italy | USA | Japan |
| Battleships | 12 | 2 | 5 | 4 | 15 | 9 |
| Battlecruisers | 3 | 2 | 1 | – | – | – |
| Pocket battleships | – | 3 | – | – | – | – |
| Cruisers | 62 | 6 | 18 | 21 | 32 | 39 |
| Aircraft carriers | 7 | – | 1 | – | 5 | 5 |
| Seaplane carriers | 2 | – | 1 | – | – | 3 |
| Destroyers | 159 | 17 | 58 | 48 | 209 | 84 |
| Torpedo boats | 11 | 16 | 13 | 69 | – | 38 |
| Submarines | 54 | 57 | 76 | 104 | 87 | 58 |
| Monitors and coast defense ships | 3 | – | – | 1 | – | 1 |
| Minelayers | 1 | – | 1 | – | 8 | 10 |
| Sloops and escort vessels | 38 | 8 | 25 | 32 | – | – |
| Gunboats and patrol vessels | 27 | – | 10 | 2 | 20 | 10 |
| Minesweepers | 38 | 29 | 8 | 39 | – | 12 |

Source: S. Roskill, *Naval Policy between the Wars* (London: Collins, 1968), Vol. 1, p. 577.

# Opening moves

*The Battle of the Atlantic was the dominating factor all through the war. Never for one moment could we forget that everything happening elsewhere, on land, at sea, or in the air, depended ultimately on its outcome, and amid all other cares we viewed its changing fortunes day by day with hope or apprehension.*

Winston Churchill

The Battle of the Atlantic was truly a decisive battle. If the Kriegsmarine had been able to achieve the same success against the merchant fleet of the British Empire as the US Navy was to achieve against that of Imperial Japan, Britain simply could not have continued the war.

There was no "phony war" at sea during World War II. The naval war was fought from the very first day to the very last. Among the first shots on September 1 during the German invasion of Poland were those fired by the 11-inch (279 mm) guns of the old German battleship *Schleswig-Holstein* against the Polish Westerplatte fortifications at Danzig. The small Polish navy was no match for the Kriegsmarine; its three serviceable destroyers escaped to Britain just before the outbreak of hostilities, while the five submarines served as a short-lived nuisance to the Germans.

On September 3 the Royal Navy sent its two famous fleet-wide telegrams, "Total Germany" and "Winston is back," announcing general hostilities and the return to the Admiralty of Winston Churchill. By this time, German surface units, their supply ships, and submarines were already in the Atlantic prepared to undertake the Kriegsmarine's anti-commerce campaign against the British Empire. However, although the *Admiral Graf Spee* and *Deutschland* had been at sea since mid-August, they did not receive orders to go into action until September 26.

While there were not yet sufficient U-boats to wage a successful submarine offensive, ominously for Britain, given its experiences of World War I, it was a U-boat that struck first. Within hours of the commencement of hostilities, *U-30* sank the liner *Athenia* with the loss of 112 lives in the mistaken belief that it was an auxiliary cruiser. Although the incident led to Admiral Raeder briefly tightening the rules of engagement, it also naturally caused the British government to believe that Germany was again conducting a strategy of unrestricted submarine warfare. In any case, by September 23 all restrictions had been lifted in the North Sea and by October 4 as far west as 15 degrees.

Winston Churchill, always eager for the offensive, ordered the formation of several submarine-hunting groups based around fleet aircraft carriers to support convoys in the Southwest Approaches. While maritime air power had played an important role in the anti-submarine effort in World War I and eventually played the decisive role in the Battle of the Atlantic, the neglect of such operations in the interwar period doomed this attempt to failure. The Fleet Air Arm did not have sufficient training, and it lacked both the equipment to find U-boats and the weaponry to destroy them.

This exercise in desperate improvisation put at serious risk the small number of almost irreplaceable carriers. On September 14 the *Ark Royal* very narrowly avoided *U-39*'s torpedoes, which went on to explode in the carrier's wake. Three days later, *Courageous* was not so fortunate when she was sunk off Ireland by two torpedoes from *U-29* with the loss of 519 of her crew. The carriers were withdrawn from anti-submarine work.

The Royal Navy's Admiralty Trade Division assumed control over British-registered shipping on August 26 and began implementing the convoy system. Only with time would they all receive a naval escort. Convoys advanced on a broad front, keeping the more valuable (and explosive) ships such as oil tankers away from the more dangerous fringes. By late 1942 a worldwide interlocking convoy system had been introduced and the convoys had increased in size after research showed that the perimeter of an 80-ship convoy was only one-seventh longer than that of a 40-ship convoy. (Topham Picturepoint)

The Kriegsmarine's U-boat arm followed this up with a daring foray into the Royal Navy's fleet base at Scapa Flow in the Orkneys, where on October 14 Gunther Prien in *U-47* penetrated a gap in the base's defenses and sank the old battleship *Royal Oak* at her moorings. It could have been worse: on October 30 *U-56* found the *Nelson*, *Rodney,* and *Hood* off Scotland. Two torpedoes actually hit *Nelson*, but they, like so many in the early months of the campaign, failed to detonate.

Meanwhile, both sides had begun laying minefields for both defensive and offensive purposes, and blockades were imposed to prevent contraband getting through. The

Germans instigated patrols in the Kattegat, Skagerrak, and Baltic, seizing over 20 ships in the second half of September alone. For Britain the blockade was its traditional strategy, although Germany was not as susceptible to a naval stranglehold this time as it had been during World War I. The southern entrance to the North Sea was easy to close, while from September 6 the Northern Patrol, made up largely of "auxiliary cruisers" – converted passenger liners – sought to prevent blockade runners from breaking through the Iceland–Orkneys gap.

By the end of October, 283 merchant ships had been stopped by the Northern Patrol, 71 of which were brought to Kirkwall in the Orkneys for inspection, resulting in the seizure of eight blockade-runners. In a bid to disrupt the patrol, in November the German battlecruisers *Scharnhorst* and *Gneisenau* sallied forth. On November 23, Captain E. C. Kennedy, RN, in the auxiliary cruiser *Rawalpindi*, sighted them, and believing that they were trying to break into the Atlantic, courageously attempted to slow them down by engaging. The unarmored,

Both Germany and Britain laid large numbers of mines for both defensive and offensive purposes. All told, some 500,000 mines were laid by all sides during World War II, using surface vessels, such as this German E-boat, submarines, or drops from the air. A variety of types were laid, including the spherical, horned contact mine and the magnetic influence variety. While they accounted for only 6.5 percent of Allied merchant traffic sunk, their presence, or suspected presence, had a huge impact on the conduct of the war at sea. (AKG London)

6-inch (152 mm) gunned, converted passenger liner was no match for the most powerful units in the German fleet and the *Rawalpindi* was sunk within 14 minutes.

## Graf Spee

When, toward the end of September, the German surface raiders *Admiral Graf Spee* and *Deutschland* (soon to be renamed *Lützow*) began offensive operations against merchant traffic, the British and French navies organized eight groups of heavy units, each known by a letter, to hunt them down in the Atlantic and Indian oceans. Unknown to the Admiralty, the *Lützow*

returned to Germany on November 8. But just after dawn on December 6, in the South Atlantic Force G, a squadron consisting of the heavy 8-inch (203 mm) cruiser *Exeter*, the light 6-inch (152 mm) cruiser *Ajax* and the New Zealand ship HMNZS *Achilles*, under Commodore Henry Harwood, encountered the *Admiral Graf Spee* off the mouth of the River Plate. The *Graf Spee*'s commanding officer, Captain Hans Langsdorff, had been under orders to avoid such encounters, and after a furious 90-minute action in which the lighter British units repeatedly closed with the heavier German vessel, the latter was forced to make for neutral Montevideo for repairs.

Unable, because of international laws restricting the presence of belligerent warships, to stay for more than 72 hours, uncertain that his ship's temperamental diesel engines would last the long, perilous voyage home, and believing a British deception that a much stronger force now awaited his vessel, Langsdorff ordered the *Graf Spee* to be scuttled in the River Plate on December 17. It was 25 years to the month since the Royal Navy had destroyed, off the

The *Graf Spee* after being scuttled on December 17, 1939, in the River Plate. She had been driven into Montevideo harbor following the action with Commodore Henry Harwood's cruiser squadron three days earlier. The *Graf Spee* was one of three *Panzerschiffe*, better known as "pocket battleships." This was a somewhat misleading description, for while her six 11-inch (279 mm) guns made her a formidable opponent, her 10,000-ton displacement was achieved at the expense of weak belt armor. (IWM A5)

Falklands, the Pacific Squadron of the German ship's namesake, Admiral Graf Spee.

The *Graf Spee* affair was brought to a conclusion when on February 16, 1940, Captain Philip Vian, RN, leading the Fourth Destroyer Flotilla in HMS *Cossack*, ignored Norwegian neutrality and patrol boats and boarded the *Altmark*, the *Graf Spee*'s supply vessel, which had illegally taken refuge in a Norwegian fjord. The 299 British prisoners taken during the *Graf Spee*'s campaign were freed.

The *Altmark* incident further concentrated the attention of both sides on Norway. Norway was vital for Germany: it protected Germany's northern flank and vital Swedish iron ore came through its coastal waters when the Baltic route was shut by winter ice. The

boarding of the *Altmark* reinforced Hitler's (justified) fears about an impending British invasion, which he now decided to pre-empt before turning his attention to the defeat of France. On April 7 the entire German fleet went to sea in 11 groups to undertake the invasions of Denmark and Norway.

## Norway

The German invasion of Norway, Operation Weserübung, heralding the first maritime campaign of World War II, began on April 9 with surprise German airborne operations to seize Norwegian airfields. Crucially, into these airfields came Luftwaffe fighters and bombers, with which German forces dominated the skies over and around Norway, frustrating attempts by the British Home Fleet under Admiral Sir Charles Forbes to intercept the German task groups.

Beyond the reach of British home-based fighter-cover, the Luftwaffe also made subsequent British and French counter-landings at a number of places in northern Norway, including Narvik and

Trondheim, even more unlikely to succeed. These hastily undertaken combined operations were a fiasco and underlined how much work still had to be done for Britain to perfect the business of amphibious warfare after so many years of willful neglect. Following the German invasions of France and the Low Countries launched on May 10, the remaining Allied forces in northern Norway began to be withdrawn.

The German occupation of Norway provided the Kriegsmarine with improved access to the North Sea and northern Atlantic, and permitted German submarine, surface, and air forces to dominate the North Cape passage to the Soviet Union. But while it also secured, as planned, Hitler's northern flank, it did not put an end to his fears of a British counterstrike there – fears that Churchill and succeeding heads of the newly established Combined Operations Headquarters sought to exploit. In a series of raids, beginning with one against the Lofoten Islands on March 3, 1941, the newly formed Commando units attacked exposed and isolated German positions, causing the Germans to divert increasing numbers of forces to protect their Scandinavian holdings.

More immediately, the experience in Norway clearly demonstrated the fallacy of the views of some leading Royal Naval officers that carrier fighter-cover was an optional extra. Literally overnight, it brought a realization in most that the fleet would find it impossible to operate in a hostile air environment. But the Royal Navy continued to suffer from the legacy of the neglect of naval aviation during the interwar period, lacking sufficient large carriers and, in particular, effective carrier-based fighters.

Even the roles that British carriers and their aircraft were capable of performing well, such as reconnaissance and anti-ship

Norway saw a series of furious naval actions. Here the German destroyer *Erich Giese* lies beached following the Second Battle of Narvik on April 13, 1940. During the battle, the Kriegsmarine lost eight modern destroyers and a submarine, while the Royal Navy suffered damage to just one destroyer. The German navy could not afford such a rate of exchange. (IWM A 21)

strikes, were of no use when assets were mishandled. On June 9 the carrier HMS *Glorious* was surprised by the German battlecruisers *Scharnhorst* and *Gneisenau* under Vice Admiral Wilhelm Marschall. The non-aviation-minded commanding officer of the carrier, Captain D'Oyly Hughes, failed to use his carrier's air group properly, which led to the wholly avoidable destruction of the carrier and her gallant escorts, HMS *Acasta* and *Ardent*, and the needless loss of over 1,400 lives in the icy waters off northern Norway.

Despite its failings, however, the Royal Navy demonstrated a determination not to yield control of the sea to the enemy, in a series of often furious actions, such as the destroyer HMS *Glowworm*'s engagement of the cruiser *Hipper* and the foray of Captain Warburton-Lee's 2nd Destroyer Flotilla up Ofotfjord to engage a much stronger German force at Narvik. In doing so, the Royal Navy exacted a heavy price from the Kriegsmarine and put a large part of the German surface fleet out of action for the rest of the year. Through both the material losses and the psychological effects, these early encounters had a telling impact on the next stages of the naval war.

## Dunkirk

With the evacuation of the Allied forces in Norway not yet complete, but with the German Blitzkrieg forcing the Allies to collapse in Belgium and France, the Royal Navy was called upon to undertake a much greater task – the evacuation of the beleaguered British Expeditionary Force from Dunkirk. This was conducted in the face of determined German air operations that eventually resulted in the loss of nine destroyers and many other craft, mostly civilian. But fortunately it was blessed with fine weather. Operation Dynamo, masterminded by Vice Admiral Bertram Ramsay at Dover, lasted from May 28 to June 4, and saw 338,226 British and French troops – but not their equipment – taken off

the moles and beaches of Dunkirk. The British Empire found itself alone.

## Indian Ocean and Red Sea, 1939–41

The Indian Ocean was the third largest theater of operations during World War II. It covers over 28 million square miles (72.5 million sq km) and contains one-fifth of the world's total sea area. Vessels that normally found themselves in coastal waters soon had to come to terms with the vast nature of the waters – the distance from Cape Town to Singapore was some 6,000 miles (9,650 km). The sea war in the Indian Ocean contained all the elements of the other theaters. Submarines, surface raiders – naval and merchant ships, German and Japanese – amphibious and carrier operations were all present. There were also a few novelties and notables. For instance, as Michael Wilson points out, "It was the one area of the world where, uniquely, the submarines of seven nations – Great Britain, the Netherlands, the United States of America, France, Italy, Germany, and Japan – all operated and fought during the war."

Yet in comparison to the other naval theaters of the Second World War, the Indian Ocean is often seen as a less important maritime battleground, playing only a supporting role to the other areas. It never saw the same fleet battles, or the same intensity of operations, as did the Atlantic, Mediterranean, and Pacific theaters. However, without unrestricted access to the Indian Ocean, British supplies to North Africa, India, and Australia, and Australian reinforcement of Britain, could not have taken place. The access that Britain enjoyed in the Indian Ocean enabled it to survive and wage war.

Had the Japanese combined their submarines and merchant raiders with Italian and German forces and attempted to cut off Allied supply lines with a degree of organization and adequate force levels, then Britain's war effort would have been crippled. Oil from the Middle East and rubber from Ceylon were two key components of the Allied war machine. Successful Axis interdiction of these sources would have undermined the war industry. The oil and rubber had to travel through the Indian Ocean and ultimately they did so remarkably unmolested. It seems the major powers directed their main efforts toward the other theaters until they could build up sufficient forces to be used constructively in the Indian Ocean.

The early years of the war in the Indian Ocean primarily revolved around safe passage for British and neutral shipping—and the attempts to stop them by the Axis forces. British units had already begun to move from the Indian Ocean to home waters at the outbreak of war, but they soon found themselves returning to the ocean to hunt down a number of German surface raiders and to escort vital convoys. The German threat was a simple yet multiple one. The German raiders comprised predominantly armed merchant ships, although the *Graf Spee* did briefly visit the Indian Ocean, accounting for a number of ships before succumbing outside Montevideo harbor. The merchant raiders all carried medium-caliber guns, but these were augmented with torpedoes, aircraft, and mines. To make matters worse, the raiders would occasionally seize merchantmen and convert them into their own auxiliaries, normally with the addition of mines. In fact, several of these ships dropped large numbers of mines off the Australian coast, resulting in serious losses, including in November 1940 the *City of Rayville*, the first American ship sunk.

Compounding the threat was the insufficient number of British convoy escorts, which remained a problem in the theater until the end of the war. Additionally, much of the non-British shipping traffic in the area often insisted on travelling independently. The British responded to the merchantmen sinkings by more patrols with ships, aircraft, and submarines. The Royal Indian Navy was also expanded to fulfill valuable escort duties, continuing to do so even when the new East Indies Fleet was created in 1944.

# Across the world's seas

## Sea Lion

Following the capitulation of France, Adolf Hitler decided to proceed with a scheme to invade Great Britain. The planning for the abortive Operation Sea Lion exposed the deep divisions within the German High Command, in particular between the head of the Luftwaffe, Herman Göring, and Eric Raeder. Despite some interest in amphibious operations in Germany prior to the war, the plan also had to contend with a total lack of preparation for what was an infinitely more demanding and complex operation than Weserübung.

However, while the Luftwaffe struggled in vain against the Royal Air Force's Fighter Command and the Channel ports filled up with hastily converted Rhine barges, Hitler began to think about the east and toward preparations for the conquest of the Soviet Union. On October 12, Sea Lion was postponed, never to be resurrected. Moreover, even had the Luftwaffe been able to wrest control of the skies from those whom Churchill described as "the few," the Kriegsmarine would still have been faced with the unenviable task of escorting the invasion convoys across the Channel in the face of what could only have been the full and furious opposition of the Royal Navy. As Admiral Raeder had cautioned, the under-strength German navy, further weakened by the Norwegian adventure, would not have been in a position to force the issue.

But the Royal Navy also found itself overstretched. It, too, had suffered losses, in both the Norwegian and Dunkirk operations. Some relief was provided by the provision of 50 old destroyers by the United States. But the navy still had to provide escorts for the convoy system, maintain its blockading operations, and be prepared to deal with German heavy units breaking out into the Atlantic, and now it had to be ready to counter the very real threat of invasion. The French collapse, of course, added to its burdens. It found itself solely responsible for the Mediterranean and, after Mussolini's decision in June "to rush to the aid of the victor," having to deal with the small—but, on paper, capable—Italian fleet, while providing support to British operations in North Africa.

In addition, although as winter approached fears of a German invasion of Britain began to recede, the U-boat menace grew. The ability of Dönitz's submarines to operate out of French Atlantic bases such as Lorient and St Nazaire meant that the Royal Navy's prewar strategy of bottling up German submarines in the North Sea had been rendered worthless, along with many of the short-range British maritime patrol aircraft and escorts.

## Wolf Pack

Dönitz's U-boats were still few in number. Indeed, given his losses and with U-boat production still at a low level, he now had fewer boats than at the beginning of the campaign. However, the French bases made the long transits into and out of the Atlantic unnecessary and thus allowed him to keep more boats in the operational area. He had experimented earlier in the war with the new strategy of attacking convoys using groups of boats, but operating closer to British home waters this technique had met with decidedly mixed success. Now, able to muster the necessary submarines on a more consistent basis and operating further out into the Atlantic, away from the attentions

of RAF Coastal Command, Dönitz's "Wolf Packs" would herald the first of his submarine service's "Happy Times."

The Wolf Pack technique worked by establishing patrol lines of submarines at right angles to the expected track of the convoy, based on information provided by the German signals intelligence organization xB-Dienst, which at this time was reading a number of British Admiralty codes, or by aerial reconnaissance. Once the convoy had been sighted by one of the patrolling submarines, its position was radioed back to U-boat Command, which would then order the pack to concentrate against the convoy. The attack usually took place at night, with the U-boats slipping inside the escort screen.

The technique relied on surface running, the submarines being fast enough (up to a maximum of around 17 knots) to enable them to outmaneuver the convoys, and also on the extensive use of radio communications. Both features were eventually exploited by the Allies to bring about the U-boats' defeat, but to begin with the Wolf Pack tactic brought Dönitz's submariners great success against a Royal

A German E-boat at high speed in the English Channel. Torpedo craft such as these, capable of speeds of around 40 knots, equipped both German and British navies and were involved in frequent and often furious engagements on the fringes of the European conflict: in the North Sea, the Channel, the Aegean, and the Black Sea. The German navy built some 250 E-boats and their main task was to attack British coastal traffic. (U-Boat Archive)

Navy that was ill-prepared to counter such an unexpected development. Toward the end of October a slow eastbound convoy, SC7, lost no fewer than 21 of its 30 ships, while a fast convoy, HX-79, following behind, had 12 out of its 49 ships sunk.

## War in the Mediterranean

The contest to dominate the Mediterranean Sea developed at a slow pace, but evolved to make this area one of the most complex and intense theaters of conflict during World War II, involving Britain, France, Germany, Greece, Italy, and the United States. The Mediterranean Sea itself represents the physical divide between the great continents of Africa, Asia, and Europe, stretching approximately 2,000

The backbone of the Kriegsmarine's U-boat arm was the Type VII submarine. These submarines were more submersible motor torpedo boats than true submarines in the modern, nuclear, sense, as they had to come to the surface regularly to recharge their electric batteries using diesel engines. On the surface, powered by their diesels, they were fast at some 17 knots, which enabled them to outmaneuver the Allies' slow merchant convoys. But when forced under water – as increasingly they were by Allied countermeasures – they were slow and had a limited endurance. (AKG Berlin)

miles (3,200 km) west to east from Gibraltar to Palestine. This consistency in length, though, is not matched by the width of the sea, which varies from 600 miles (1,000 km) to less than 100 miles (160 km) in certain places, such as the gap between Tunisia and Sicily. The strategic significance of this enclosed sea had been transformed in the nineteenth century by the construction of the Suez Canal in Egypt, which considerably reduced the distance for ships travelling to the Far East. The Cape route was a 13,000 mile (21,000 km) trip. As such, it became a sea-lane of vital importance to colonial powers like Britain.

The pace of conflict in this theater accelerated dramatically after the fall of France (with all its colonies in North Africa) to victorious German forces on June 22, 1940, and Italy's entry into the war in the same month. At this time, Britain's position in the Mediterranean could hardly have been worse. As a nation, it was struggling to contain the threat from Germany, conducting the humiliating withdrawal from Dunkirk and the desperate Battle of Britain. At sea, the German navy had stretched the Royal Navy to the limit in the Atlantic Ocean, using a handful of major units such as the *Admiral Graf Spee*, U-boats, and maritime aircraft. Now Britain was required somehow to neutralize the latent threat from the French naval forces based in North Africa and to cope with a new foe, Italy.

Britain's interests in the region were centered on three strategic locations: Egypt, Gibraltar, and Malta. Fortunately for the Royal Navy, it possessed one of its ablest commanders as Commander-in-Chief, Mediterranean Fleet, Admiral Sir Andrew

Admiral Sir Andrew Browne Cunningham, or A.B.C. to his friends, was arguably the finest naval commander in the Royal Navy throughout World War II. In terms of character, he was a fiery and aggressive man who always tried to seek out and destroy the enemy whenever possible. Under his command, the Mediterranean Fleet achieved the stunning victories at Taranto and Matapan as well as keeping the supply line to Malta open. He was appointed First Sea Lord in October 1943. (IWM MH 31338)

Browne Cunningham. Cunningham's fleet, based at Alexandria rather than the more vulnerable Malta (the traditional base of the Royal Navy) was somewhat small in terms of capital ships in the summer of 1940. It possessed just four old battleships – HMS *Warspite* (flagship), HMS *Malaya*, HMS *Royal Sovereign,* and HMS *Valiant* (arrived August 1940) – the aircraft carrier HMS *Eagle*, and five light cruisers as well as 17 destroyers.

At Gibraltar, Britain's naval forces were designated "Force H" under the command of Vice Admiral Sir James Somerville. Its composition changed significantly with, and at one stage included, the famous battlecruiser HMS *Hood*. By August 1940, it comprised the battleship HMS *Resolution*, the battlecruiser HMS *Renown*, the aircraft carrier HMS *Ark Royal*, a cruiser, and seven destroyers.

HMS *Warspite* was a Queen Elizabeth–class battleship, commissioned in 1915 and a veteran of the First World War. She had been modernized in 1936 in vital areas such as engines, armor, armament, and the elevation of her powerful 15-inch (381 mm) guns, which had a 32,000-yard (29,260 meter) range. By 1940 this ship could only make 24 knots at most, which was considerably slower than more modern battleships that could make up to 30 knots. (IWM A20652)

Vice Admiral Sir James Somerville was a popular and highly effective commander of Force H. The demands on his unit were enormous due to its Atlantic and Mediterranean responsibilities, from helping to sink the *Bismarck* off the coast of France on May 27, 1941, to escorting supply convoys to Malta. Somerville was subsequently promoted to full admiral and took charge of the battered Eastern Fleet in February 1942. (IWM A30166 WA)

In bomb-strewn Malta, defenses were extremely run down by mid-1940 with just a handful of Sea Gladiator fighters, nicknamed "Faith," "Hope," and "Charity," and 38 anti-aircraft guns. The significance of Malta lay in its location between Sicily and the North African coast as well as in the ships, and particularly the submarines, that operated from it.

## Oran and Mers-el-Kebir

The fall of France in June 1940 and the subsequent accession to power of the Vichy regime under Marshal Pétain put French naval forces in North Africa in a difficult position. French colonies extended from Dakar in French West Africa to parts of Morocco, Algeria, and Tunisia, and the naval forces on station at the time were sizable. In the Algerian ports of Oran and Mers-el-Kebir were four battleships, 13 destroyers, one seaplane carrier, and four submarines; at Dakar there were two new battleships; and at Alexandria, under British guns, one battleship with four cruisers. After the capitulation of France, the Commander-in-Chief of the French navy, Admiral Darlan, made it clear that French naval forces would not be handed over to any foreign power without a fight. However, his acceptance of a position in the Vichy government on June 27, 1940, raised doubts about the future of the French fleet.

Italy's position after June 10, 1940, was more clear-cut. It had colonies in Libya, Somaliland, and Abyssinia (Ethiopia), and mustered 500,000 troops in total, including powerful naval forces (Regia Marina) supported by an air force (Regia Aeronautica) of more than 1,200 aircraft. The Italian forces in Libya under Marshal Graziani enjoyed overwhelming superiority over their British counterparts, and appeared likely (on paper at least) to dominate the region in the short to medium term. Germany's initial commitment to North Africa was small in number but significant in terms of quality. Fliegerkorps X (a specialist anti-ship squadron of the Luftwaffe) was deployed to Italy in December 1940, U-boats were made available in small numbers, and General Erwin Rommel and the Afrika Korps were deployed to Libya in February 1941.

The potential threat of the French naval forces in North Africa forced the British Prime Minister and the First Sea Lord to order Force H to execute the infamous Operation Catapult, or the destruction of the French forces at Mers-el-Kebir, on July 3, 1940. This highly unpleasant action took place after the failure of British negotiations with the local French commander, Admiral Gensoul. Two French battleships, *Dunkerque* and *Provence*, were seriously damaged (along with the seaplane carrier *Commandante Teste*), the *Bretagne* blew up, and the *Strasbourg* managed to escape to Toulon. A total of 1,250 French sailors were killed in this operation. Five days later, British forces attacked Dakar and put the battleship

General Erwin Rommel was one of the best military leaders of the entire war. As an officer, he possessed the rare "common touch" with his troops, to whom he was an inspiration. For the British and Commonwealth soldiers who faced the Afrika Korps in the early years of the war, his presence and actions generated the idea that he was some kind of "superman." (IWM)

two forces converged and the 7th British Cruiser Squadron, under Vice Admiral J. C. Tovey, made the famous signal "Enemy battle fleet in sight." HMS *Warspite* exchanged salvoes with the Italian battleship *Giulio Cesare*, causing such damage that the Italian Admiral Riccardi made smoke and retreated successfully away from the British forces.

Despite excellent work by the aircraft of HMS *Eagle*, which sank a destroyer, Cunningham could not consolidate his tactical success because of a lack of speed in his capital ships; his old battleships were simply too slow to catch the escaping Italians. However, the lessons from this action were clear: the aggressive ethos of the Royal Navy made up for the technological and numerical superiority of the Italian navy, whose will to fight appeared fragile at best.

## Taranto

One of the most significant military strikes in the early years of the war in the Mediterranean was the raid on Taranto, or Operation Judgement, carried out by aircraft of the Fleet Air Arm (FAA) on November 11, 1940. The plan of striking at the heart of the Italian fleet in the massive naval base of Taranto was devised by Rear Admiral Lyster and was warmly accepted by Cunningham. The original plan called for strikes from two aircraft carriers, but mechanical problems with HMS *Eagle* forced the Royal Navy to rely on just one carrier.

Sailing with an escort of five battleships, two cruisers, and 13 destroyers, HMS *Illustrious* launched the strike at 170 miles (275 km) distance from Taranto. In two waves, 21 Swordfish aircraft flew toward Taranto early that evening and found six Italian battleships and some cruisers and destroyers calmly at

*Richelieu* out of action. In stark contrast, at Alexandria, Cunningham (who opposed using force against the French) managed to persuade Admiral Godfroy to disarm his vessels by removing vital parts without a shot being fired.

The first major action between the British Mediterranean Fleet and the Italian navy occurred off the coast of Calabria on July 9, 1940, and revealed a pattern of warfare that was to repeat itself continually throughout the war. Cunningham took the British fleet at sea to cover a British convoy from Malta to Gibraltar, but received information while under way that a convoy of ships was heading from Italy to Libya; in typical fashion, he turned to engage the enemy. Protecting the Italian convoy was a strong force of two battleships, a dozen or more cruisers, and a multitude of destroyers.

On July 8, 1940, the Regia Aeronautica first attacked the British fleet from the air, but they only managed to damage the cruiser HMS *Gloucester* despite launching several waves of attacks. The next day the

To Mussolini (shown above, left) and the Italian navy, the Mediterranean was *mare nostrum* (our sea). In just one night, the balance of power shifted dramatically in favor of the Royal Navy, but more importantly a huge psychological blow was inflicted on the greatly reduced fleet of Admiral Cavagnari, the Commander-in-Chief of the Italian navy. Taranto was a revolutionary moment in naval history: it heralded the replacement of the battleship by the aircraft carrier as the capital ship of the sea. (NYP 68066)

anchor. The damage inflicted by the first operational strike of this kind in naval history was spectacular: the battleship *Conte di Cavour* was sunk in the harbor (despite being recovered, it was never operational again in the war); the *Littorio* (renamed *Italia*) suffered three torpedo hits, while another torpedo hit the *Caio Diulio*; and the heavy cruiser *Trento* also sustained damage along with a few destroyers and the oil facilities. Operation Judgement cost the Royal Navy just two aircraft.

## Logistics in the Mediterranean

The war in the Mediterranean Sea was, largely, a war of logistics. The problems involved in supplying ground forces in North Africa dominated the military strategies of all three major protagonists in the Mediterranean theater, Britain, Italy, and Germany. The only method of transporting bulk supplies, troops, and tanks was the escorted convoy, since transport aircraft could provide only a fraction of what sea-based methods offered. Consequently, maritime operations were centered on convoy and anti-convoy operations.

British efforts in this area entailed huge amounts of resources from Force H and the Mediterranean fleet to keep the supply lines open from the home base to Egypt (the only other major front against Germany until 1943) via Gibraltar and Malta. The list of such operations is extensive, including Operation Hurry in early August 1940 (12 Hurricane air defense fighters, transported to Malta) and Operation Coat in mid-November 1940 (only four out of 12 Hurricanes made it to Malta; the rest crashed into the sea). The most famous of the British convoys was undoubtedly Operation Pedestal in August 1942.

For the German and Italian convoys to Libya, Malta was to prove a painful thorn in the side of their overall strategy. In the same manner that German and Italian submarines preyed on the convoys from Alexandria, British submarines attacked these slow convoys carrying vital supplies to Rommel's army in the North African desert. Air power was particularly valuable in finding and sinking convoys on both sides; the German Luftwaffe demonstrated considerable skill in this art, either through direct attack or mining operations in the Suez Canal.

# The Mediterranean

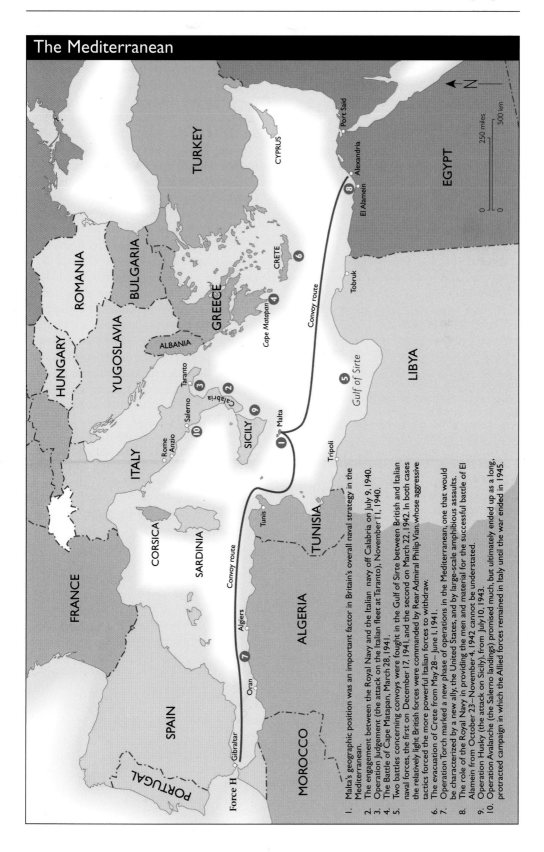

1.  Malta's geographic position was an important factor in Britain's overall naval strategy in the Mediterranean.
2.  The engagement between the Royal Navy and the Italian navy off Calabria on July 9, 1940.
3.  Operation Judgement (the attack on the Italian fleet at Taranto), November 11, 1940.
4.  The Battle of Cape Matapan, March 28, 1941.
5.  Two battles concerning convoys were fought in the Gulf of Sirte between British and Italian naval forces, the first on December 17, 1941, and the second on March 22, 1942. In both cases the relatively light British forces were commanded by Rear Admiral Philip Vian, whose aggressive tactics forced the more powerful Italian forces to withdraw.
6.  The evacuation of Crete from May 28–June 1, 1941.
7.  Operation Torch marked a new phase of operations in the Mediterranean, one that would be characterized by a new ally, the United States, and by large-scale amphibious assaults.
8.  The role of the Royal Navy in providing the men and material for the successful battle of El Alamein from October 23–November 4, 1942 cannot be understated.
9.  Operation Husky (the attack on Sicily), from July 10, 1943.
10. Operation Avalanche (the Salerno landings) promised much, but ultimately ended up as a long, protracted campaign in which the Allied forces remained in Italy until the war ended in 1945.

## Red Sea, 1940–41

*Operation Pedestal*

Operation Pedestal, from August 13, 1942, involved two battleships, three fleet aircraft carriers with 72 aircraft, seven cruisers, and 24 destroyers, transporting 36 Spitfires in another aircraft carrier to Malta, together with 14 vital merchant ships under the command of Rear Admiral E. N. Syfret. The cost was enormous: one aircraft carrier, HMS *Eagle*, was sunk and one seriously damaged; two cruisers were destroyed and one was crippled, with the Italian submarine *Axum* accounting for two of the cruiser hits; one destroyer was sunk and one crippled; and nine of the precious merchant ships were sunk as well.

In the short term, the threat to merchant shipping in the Indian Ocean appeared to worsen in June 1940 with the entry of Italy into the war. Italy had a number of submarines and large escort vessels based in Massawa, its main port in Eritrea on the Red Sea. Although these Italian units were now cut off due to the closure of the Suez Canal, initially they posed a major threat. Quite rapidly this situation changed, however, as the Italian vessels accounted for only a handful of British merchant ships. Convoys were soon running the gauntlet through the Red Sea to the Suez Canal and back again with a large degree of impunity. Most of the Italian submarines could not operate in the narrows of the Red Sea without problems, and they all suffered from high temperatures in the crew compartments. The submarines were also relatively unwilling to venture too far into the Indian Ocean, where the hunting was easier.

Gradually, through a combination of British air strikes, convoy escorts, and poor supply, most of the Italian vessels in the Red Sea had

The most famous British submarine commander was Lieutenant Commander M. D. Wanklyn VC, who commanded HMS *Upholder*. This submarine sank two Italian troop-carrying ships, the 19,500-ton *Neptunia* and *Oceania* on September 18, 1941. Between June and September 1941, British submarines sank 150,000 tons of enemy shipping. (IWM A7293)

been lost by the start of 1941. Nevertheless, they remained a threat to the ongoing land campaign in east Africa. The Royal Navy had already carried out an evacuation of troops in 1940, but it was now acting in support of the renewed land war against the Italians in east Africa. This conflict had turned in favor of Britain, and a combination of British victory in the region and a powerful Royal Navy made it only a matter of time before the Italian naval bases were overrun.

The Italian Naval Command decided that the remaining Italian surface ships should attempt a surprise raid on British forces, while the Italian submarines were to travel the 13,000 miles (21,000 km) around Africa to the safety of German-held France. En route they were to be replenished by German support ships and merchant raiders. When starting this mission, the Italian surface ships were intercepted by British naval forces, but amazingly the four Italian submarines that set off on their grueling journey to France all succeeded in reaching their destination.

This propaganda coup for Italy actually meant increased safety for British shipping for the remainder of 1941 in the Red Sea and Indian Ocean. It also meant that, now that the Italian presence was no longer a nuisance, supplies could flow to Egypt and to the war effort in North Africa much more easily. But the respite was short and was over by the end of the year. The war clouds in the east were continuing to gather, and the vulnerability of all British possessions east of Suez was obvious to all.

## Matapan

The success of the Royal Navy in the Mediterranean, just as in the Atlantic theater, was aided by the use of intelligence through decrypted intercepts of enemy communications traffic (Enigma). Such information provided Cunningham with his finest moment in the Mediterranean campaign, the Battle of Cape Matapan on March 28, 1941.

The Italian fleet comprised one battleship, *Vittorio Veneto*, with 15-inch (381 mm) guns; six heavy cruisers, *Pola, Fiume, Trieste, Trento, Bolzano*, and *Zara*, with 8-inch (203 mm) guns; two light cruisers with 6-inch (152 mm) guns; and 13 destroyers under Admiral Iachino, which had set sail in three groups to intercept the British "Lustre" convoys ferrying troops to Greece. Cunningham steamed from Alexandria to intercept the Italians with three battleships (HMS *Warspite*, HMS *Barham*, and HMS *Valiant*), one aircraft carrier (HMS *Formidable*), and nine destroyers. In support of Cunningham, his second-in-command, Rear Admiral H. D. Pridham-Wippell, moved to a position ahead of the main force; he had four cruisers with 6-inch (152 mm) guns and nine destroyers.

On the morning of March 28, he encountered three Italian heavy cruisers and outgunned, he attempted to draw them toward the British battleships some 80 miles (130 km) away. Cunningham realized that he had to slow down the Italians in order for his old battleships to catch up, so around midday HMS *Formidable* launched air strikes. Five Fleet Air Arm aircraft managed to get one hit on the Italian battleship, reducing her speed to just 15 knots, and another air strike that evening crippled the cruiser *Pola*. Hoping to have caught the battleship, which had in fact escaped, Cunningham steamed toward the *Pola*, which was now surrounded by two other cruisers and two destroyers.

The Italian ships were completely unaware of the presence of the British battleships until the opening salvoes at a deadly range of fewer than 4,000 yards (3,660 m). Two cruisers, *Fiume* and *Zara*, disintegrated under the weight of fire in just five minutes. Two supporting destroyers went down as well, and five hours later the *Pola* was sunk. In all, 2,400 Italian sailors were killed, including the commanding officer, Vice Admiral Cattaneo. To some, the Battle of Cape Matapan represented the greatest British naval victory at sea since Trafalgar, but above all things it cemented the superiority of the Royal Navy over the Italian navy.

## Red Sea

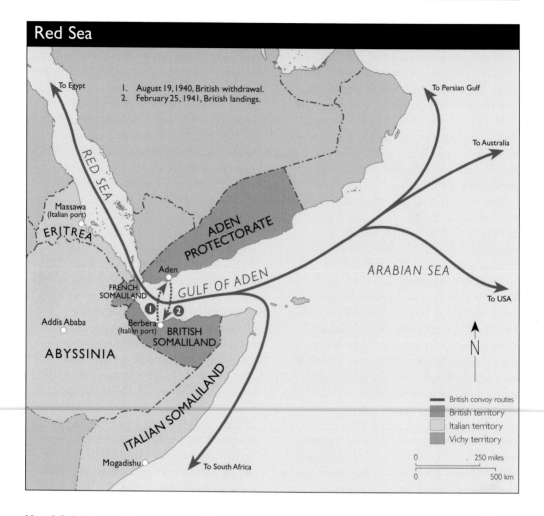

1. August 19, 1940, British withdrawal.
2. February 25, 1941, British landings.

To Egypt

To Persian Gulf

To Australia

RED SEA

Massawa
(Italian port)

ERITREA

ADEN PROTECTORATE

To USA

Aden

ARABIAN SEA

FRENCH SOMALILAND

GULF OF ADEN

Addis Ababa

Berbera
(Italian port)

BRITISH SOMALILAND

ABYSSINIA

ITALIAN SOMALILAND

N

Mogadishu

To South Africa

British convoy routes
British territory
Italian territory
Vichy territory

0      250 miles
0      500 km

Mussolini's decision to declare war on a statistically weaker Britain in the Mediterranean may have seemed a worthwhile gamble. However, it meant that the Red Sea forces were cut off from Italy and their supplies. Unless Italy could defeat British forces in Egypt and east Africa, its isolated naval garrison would eventually succumb to an overwhelming Royal Navy presence. Initially, Italy held the advantage over the British Empire on the land in east Africa, forcing an amphibious withdrawal. However, the same naval flexibility enabled British forces to come back into east Africa and ensured eventual victory in 1941 and the seizure of the Italian ports.

## Crete

If Cape Matapan was the high point for the Royal Navy then the withdrawal of British troops from Crete was the low point. Churchill's disastrous decision to reallocate resources from the highly successful British

and Commonwealth ground forces in Libya, which had virtually defeated the Italian army, in order to defend Greece and Crete was one of the defining moments of the Mediterranean campaign. The collapse of these redeployed forces in Greece and Crete, and the subsequent evacuations (April 24–29 and May 28–June 1, 1941, respectively) cost the Mediterranean Fleet off Crete dearly: two damaged battleships, one aircraft carrier, three sunk cruisers (five damaged), and six sunk destroyers (seven damaged); however, 18,000 troops had been saved.

This devastating year for the Royal Navy was capped by a group of daring Italian frogmen who sneaked into Alexandria harbor on "human chariots" (small underwater vehicles) and, using explosive charges, holed the battleships HMS *Queen*

*Elizabeth* and HMS *Valiant* on December 19, 1941. In effect, this act neutralized the remaining heavy units of the Mediterranean Fleet, which was now down to just three cruisers and a small collection of destroyers.

## Bismarck

During the winter of 1940, the German heavy units once again forayed out into the Atlantic. *Admiral Scheer* reached the Atlantic at the beginning of November, attacking the 42-ship convoy HX-84, escorted by the auxiliary cruiser *Jervis Bay*. The latter, before she could be sunk, gave her merchant charges sufficient time for all but five to escape. *Admiral Scheer* then proceeded to the South Atlantic and Indian Ocean before returning home in April 1941 having sunk 17 ships. In early December 1940, her sister ship, *Admiral Hipper,* made the first of two deployments in the Atlantic before reaching Norway in the spring of 1941. By then the *Scharnhorst* and *Gneisenau* had reached the Atlantic, and during February and March they sank or captured 22 ships, preying on those from recently dispersed convoys. On March 23, the German battlecruisers reached Brest.

It was intended that both Brest-based ships would join the 42,000-ton battleship *Bismarck* and the heavy cruiser *Prinz Eugen*, both newly commissioned, and seven tankers and other support ships, in the most ambitious commercial raiding operation planned by the Kriegsmarine. However, the damage caused by repeated air attacks by RAF Bomber Command on Brest prevented this. Consequently, Operation Rheinübung began on May 18 with only the *Bismarck* and *Prinz Eugen* moving to sea from their bases in Gotenhafen and Kiel.

Initially spotted by a Swedish cruiser in the Kattegat and detected by an RAF photo-reconnaissance Spitfire refueling in Grimstad fjord, south of Bergen, they headed north. Thus, with the Royal Navy so badly mauled in the Mediterranean, the most powerful battleship in the world was on the loose in the Atlantic shipping lanes. The Denmark Strait and the Iceland–Shetland gap were patrolled by several cruisers backed up by Admiral Holland's battlegroup of HMS *Hood* and the newly commissioned battleship HMS *Prince of Wales*, which still had civilian shipyard workers on board. Meanwhile, the Commander-in-Chief Home Fleet, Admiral John Tovey, left Scapa Flow on board the *Prince of Wales*'s sister ship, *King George V*, accompanied by the carrier *Victorious*.

On the evening of May 23, the German ships were spotted by the heavy cruisers *Norfolk* and *Suffolk* in the Denmark Strait. Using radar, the British ships tracked the *Bismarck* and *Prinz Eugen* as they headed south into the northern Atlantic; position reports were sent to the closing *Hood* and *Prince of Wales*, which came in sight of their adversaries at dawn the next day. At 5:52 am the *Hood* opened up, but the reply of the German ships was immediate and accurate, hitting *Hood* with their first salvoes. Her armor was penetrated and her aft magazine exploded, followed almost immediately by her forward magazine. *Hood* sank at once, with only three of her crew of 1,420 surviving. After taking a number of hits, the *Prince of Wales* managed to disengage, joining *Norfolk* and *Suffolk* in shadowing the German ships.

The encounter had left the *Bismarck* with a small oil leak and a reduction in speed. A highly satisfied Admiral Lütjens decided to make for Brest. Meanwhile, the Admiralty mobilized every available ship to converge on Lütjens' flagship, including Admiral Somerville's Force H from the Mediterranean. Nineteen capital ships, carriers, and cruisers, and almost as many destroyers were to hunt the *Bismarck* down.

After a vain attack by Swordfish torpedo bombers and Fulmar fighters from *Victorious*, the *Prinz Eugen* split from the *Bismarck* in order to operate independently in the Atlantic. The *Bismarck* managed for a while to give the Royal Navy the slip too. However, as she headed for the French coast she was detected once again, her position confirmed at 10:30 am on May 26 by an RAF Coastal Command Catalina flying boat 700 miles (1,125 km) west of Brest. Tovey's Home Fleet was not able to intercept, but at 9:00 pm that evening a force of Swordfish led by Lieutenant T. P. Goode from Force H's carrier *Ark Royal* managed to disable the *Bismarck's* steering gear. After being harried by British destroyers during the night, shortly before 9:00 am on May 27, the *Bismarck* was engaged by Tovey's main force, including the battleships *King George V* and *Rodney* and the cruisers *Dorsetshire* and *Norfolk*. After surviving 109 minutes of bombardment, the *Bismarck* was finished off by torpedoes from the *Dorsetshire*. Only 109 of her crew were saved.

It has been argued that the winter of 1940–41 was the only time that the Germans could have achieved victory in the Atlantic campaign. Despite efforts by the British to

The *Bismarck* engaging HMS *Hood*, May 24, 1941. The destruction of the Royal Navy's mighty battlecruiser was a major blow to Great Britain and led to a huge naval operation to hunt down the German battleship. (IWM HU382)

extend the range of their anti-submarine efforts both at and over the sea, which did push the submarines further west, the Royal Navy and RAF Coastal Command lacked both adequate tactics and equipment to successfully counter the Wolf Pack attacks. But Dönitz lacked sufficient numbers of submarines and as 1941 progressed he was also forced, to his considerable frustration, to divert increasing numbers of submarines to northern operations in support of Operation Barbarossa and during the autumn to the Mediterranean to combat the Royal Navy there.

## Allied improvements in the Atlantic

By this time the British had also begun reading the U-boat ciphered radio traffic with increasing regularity and speed, which continued until February 1942, when the design of the submarines' Enigma machines was improved. This effort was aided by the Royal Navy's capture of a number of Enigma code machines. Among these was *U-110's* machine, seized by a boarding party led by

sublieutenant David Balme, which was put aboard from HMS *Bulldog* on May 9, 1941. They recovered the priceless machine after overpowering the crew of the sinking submarine. The prodigious efforts of the British code-breakers at the Government Code and Cipher School at Bletchley Park did not provide information sufficient to target individual submarines, although the surface supply vessels and, later, the specialist Type XIV resupply submarines, the so-called *Milchkühe*, were vulnerable. Crucially, however, the information did allow the rerouting of convoys away from known concentrations of U-boats.

In February 1941, Western Approaches Command was moved from Plymouth to Liverpool, where the majority of convoys were now routed. Initially under the command of Admiral Sir Percy Noble, from November 1942, it was led by Admiral Sir Max Horton, who had won fame for his exploits as a submariner in World War I. From April 1941 the new headquarters benefited from the Admiralty being given operational control over the activities of RAF Coastal Command. Derby House was responsible for the allocation of escorts and the routing of convoys based on intelligence information it received from the Admiralty's Operational Intelligence Centre's Submarine Tracking Room. Also to be located in Liverpool was the Western Approaches Tactical Unit (WATU), which, taking its cue from the work of individual anti-submarine escort commanders such as Commander Frederick Walker, was responsible for developing an increasingly effective anti-submarine tactical doctrine.

By the spring of 1941, the British were also making very efficient use of their shipping resources and through rationing had reduced their import, and therefore tonnage, requirements. In fact, during 1941 import requirements were running at about half the prewar rate. A major shipbuilding program was also progressing: in 1941 British yards launched 1.2 million tons, with another 7 million tons on order from American yards. So, despite the fact that

the year saw 3.6 million tons sunk, Britain ended 1941 with an increase in tonnage. Submarines accounted for 2.1 million tons of the losses, the rest being caused by single merchant raiders, the Luftwaffe, and Admiral Raeder's surface raiders.

The year 1941 saw the increasing participation of the United States – long before its official involvement following the Japanese attack on Pearl Harbor. In April 1941 Britain had established air and escort bases on Iceland, which enabled the smaller escorts to operate out to around 35° west. Following the meeting between Churchill and President Roosevelt at Placentia Bay in August 1941, the United States took responsibility for the western Atlantic, including Iceland, and from mid-September the US Navy began to escort fast convoys between there and North America. During one of these operations, on October 31, the American destroyer *Reuben James* was sunk by *U-552* with the loss of 100 sailors while escorting convoy HX-156. This was the first US Navy ship to be sunk. The slow convoys became the responsibility of the Royal Canadian Navy but, laboring with often badly trained crews and denied adequate equipment, its performance was poor.

## Indian Ocean, 1942

At the start of 1942 the Royal Navy and Churchill were still assessing the impact of the loss of HMS *Prince of Wales* and HMS *Repulse* to Japanese aircraft in December 1941. By the spring of 1942, however, the Eastern Fleet, under the command of Admiral Somerville, became operational in the Indian Ocean. The fleet's main aims were to stop any major incursions into the ocean by Japanese forces and to defend British territories and convoys.

On paper, Somerville's force was impressive, with five battleships, three aircraft carriers, and numerous escorts. However, only one of the battleships had been modernized and the carriers possessed far fewer aircraft, and these of generally worse quality, than the Japanese.

Moved to Derby House in Liverpool in February 1941, Western Approaches Command was responsible for the allocation of escorts and the routing of convoys based on intelligence information it received from the Admiralty's Operational Intelligence Center's Submarine Tracking Room. From April 1941 it also had operational control over the activities of RAF Coastal Command. Under Admiral Sir Max Horton it would help to achieve victory in the Battle of the Atlantic. (IWM A 25746)

Additionally, there were insufficient anti-aircraft weapons in the fleet and the naval bases in Ceylon were too vulnerable to air attack. A refueling base at Addu Atoll provided some sanctuary from attack, but little in the way of fleet support.

Admiral Somerville and London were determined that he would not lose his command in the same fashion as the *Prince of Wales* and the *Repulse*. Consequently, no direct action against the Japanese was to take place. However, in April 1942, a sizable Japanese fleet entered the Indian Ocean with five aircraft carriers and four battleships. In the first weeks of April, the Japanese fleet attacked Ceylon, India, and shipping, inflicting heavy British losses, including the cruisers *Cornwall* and *Dorsetshire* and the aircraft carrier *Hermes*.

Somerville was then directed to remove his weakest ships to the western Indian Ocean. Britain had reached its lowest ebb in the Indian Ocean. Unable to defend India and Ceylon, and having lost Singapore and Burma, the Royal Navy was forced to establish a presence in the Indian Ocean as a potential barrier to Japan's ambitions until such time as the Eastern Fleet could be built up.

## Arctic convoys

Although the increasing involvement of the United States in the Atlantic was welcome, it did little to lift the burdens on the Royal Navy, to which, in August 1941, was added responsibility for protecting the Arctic convoys. Following the German invasion of the Soviet Union, on June 22, 1941, Britain sought to supply its new ally. The first convoy left Scapa Flow on August 21, 1941. Eventually, almost a quarter of the total lend-lease supplies sent to Russia, nearly 4.5 million tons of weapons, trucks, aircraft, and equipment, were carried along this

## Japanese incursions in the Indian Ocean

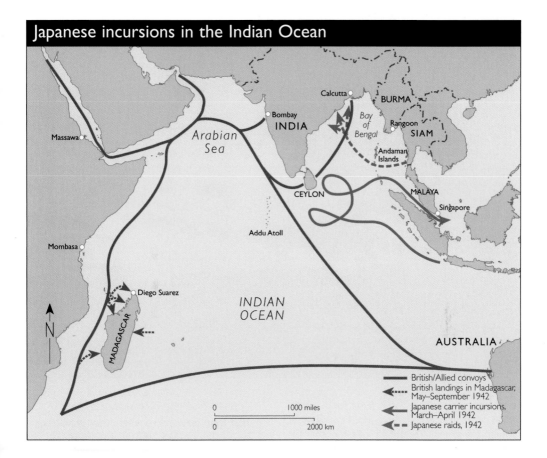

dangerous North Cape convoy route. Almost 8 percent of the merchant ships sent never arrived at their destinations of Murmansk, Archangel, or Molotovsk.

The convoy routes were constrained by both geography and weather. Winter found ice forcing the convoys closer to the Norwegian coast, but at least provided the cover of the long Arctic nights. Ships and their crews had to contend with heavy seas and the extreme cold. If it was not removed, ships could accumulate dangerous coverings of ice. In the water, without modern survival aids, survivors of sinkings had little chance. However, until March 1942 the Germans did not expend much effort against the Arctic convoys.

## Operation Drumbeat

Ironically, the formal entry of the United States into the war brought no respite – only greatly increased danger. Ignoring the lessons of history, in particular those of World War I and British experience in World War II, the US Navy's Chief of Naval Operations, Admiral King, refused to implement a convoy system off the eastern seaboard, relying instead on offensive patrols and protected sea lanes. In an operation code-named "Drumbeat" from January 1942, Dönitz began concentrating his submarines off the American coast, where they preyed on individual sailing ships that were often illuminated by the unextinguished lights of the coastal towns and highways. In May and June alone, the U-boats sank over one million tons of shipping in these waters. This was the German submarine service's second "Happy Time."

Only as an American convoy system was increasingly introduced and more escorts were made available – including some 20 transferred from Britain and Canada – did

HMS *Hermes* was the Royal Navy's first purpose-built aircraft carrier. She also became the first British carrier to be sunk by air power, on April 9, 1942. Without her air group, or land-based air cover, the *Hermes* was assaulted by aircraft from the Japanese carriers of the 1st Carrier Fleet. Following some 40 hits and near misses, she sank off Ceylon with the loss of over 300 men. The presence of her air group would have made little difference, since it comprised only Swordfish torpedo bomber aircraft and not fighters for air defense. (IWM HU 1839)

the losses fall off, forcing Dönitz's submarines to move elsewhere, initially to the Caribbean. However, with a global system of interlocking convoys now in place and more extensive and effective Allied air patrols, his submarines were finding it harder to locate areas in which they could easily operate.

## The Channel Dash

While Dönitz's submarines were wreaking havoc in the American shipping lanes in early 1942, Hitler was becoming alarmed at the possibility of an Allied invasion of Norway. The battlecruisers *Scharnhorst* and *Gneisenau*, and

the cruiser *Prinz Eugen*, were then at Brest. Rather than leave them where they posed a considerable threat to the Atlantic shipping lanes, in a misguided effort to shore up his Scandinavian defenses Hitler ordered them to break out for Norway via the English Channel. This operation – code-named "Cerberus" by the Germans – was deemed so risky by Admiral Raeder that he refused to accept any responsibility for it.

However, through a series of failures, both technical and human, on the part of the Royal Air Force and the Royal Navy, the Admiralty was not alerted to the fact that the German squadron was at sea on February 11 until it was too late to mount a successful interception. It was only possible to launch small, uncoordinated, and in the case of a Swordfish attack by six aircraft – all of which were lost – virtually suicidal attacks. The German ships managed to reach Germany, to the considerable embarrassment of the British and the understandable glee of their opponents. Nevertheless, both battlecruisers were damaged by British air-dropped mines, and the *Gneisenau* was subsequently damaged beyond

In September 1940 the British ordered 60 ships from yards in the United States in a simple British design. To speed up their manufacture further, the Americans modified the design, dispensing with rivets in favor of welding. In January 1941, the United States ordered 200 7,126-ton ships based on the modified British design to meet its own emergency shipbuilding program, the "Liberty Fleet." Eventually, 2,710 Liberty ships would be constructed, about 200 going to Britain, mostly by the Kaiser shipyards, using a mass-production system that on one occasion saw a vessel launched just four days and 15½ hours after the keel had been laid. (IWM A23033)

repair in a bombing raid on her dry-dock. It was March 1943 before the *Scharnhorst* arrived in Norway.

## Return to the Arctic

From March 1942, their expected quick victory against the Soviets not having materialized, German forces began to concentrate in northern Norway in a bid to stop the increasing amount of supplies reaching the Eastern Front. Convoys had initially sailed with a close escort of destroyers and smaller ships and a distant escort of cruisers. But after March 1942 heavy units of the Home Fleet provided more distant cover to guard against the German heavy units, including the *Bismarck's* sister ship the *Tirpitz*, lying in wait in the Norwegian fjords.

However, opposition increasingly came from the Luftwaffe. On May 27, 1942, convoy PQ16 was attacked by no fewer than 108 aircraft. A total of seven ships were eventually lost from this convoy. The next convoy, PQ17, left Iceland on June 27, 1942. After Ultra intelligence was received that it was about to be attacked by a strong German force, which potentially included the *Tirpitz*,

the cruisers *Hipper* and *Admiral Scheer*, and the pocket battleship *Lützow*, convoy PQ17 was ordered by the Admiralty to scatter. The dispersed ships were instead attacked from the air, and only 11 out of the convoy's 37 merchant ships reached their destination. A total of 153 seamen died, and 2,500 aircraft, over 400 tanks, and almost 4,000 other vehicles were lost. This disaster and the demands of the Mediterranean theater largely forced the suspension of the Arctic convoys until December 1942, much to the annoyance of Stalin.

## Madagascar

The Vichy French island of Madagascar had worried the Allies since late 1941 with the

## Eastern Indian Ocean – sinkings and incursions

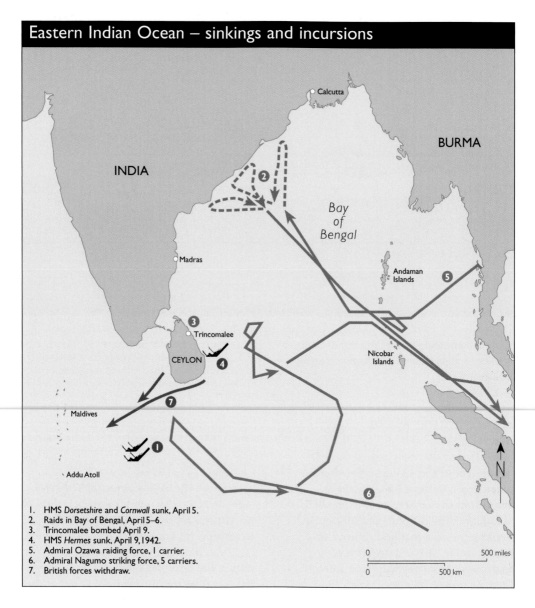

1. HMS *Dorsetshire* and *Cornwall* sunk, April 5.
2. Raids in Bay of Bengal, April 5–6.
3. Trincomalee bombed April 9.
4. HMS *Hermes* sunk, April 9, 1942.
5. Admiral Ozawa raiding force, 1 carrier.
6. Admiral Nagumo striking force, 5 carriers.
7. British forces withdraw.

Japanese war in the Pacific. It stood near the route to the Middle East and India, via the Southern African Cape, and could be used easily by Japanese submarines as a base to cut these vital supply lines. Thus Operation Ironclad was initiated to neutralize and occupy the island. The operation was so secret that not even the Free French were told of its existence until the operation had commenced.

A substantial force was assembled, with ships being taken from home waters and Force H. Rear Admiral Syfret of Force H was in command. This was the first large amphibious operation since the Norway and Dakar missions of 1940. Following their sailing from Durban at the start of the month, 13,000 British Empire troops landed in Madagascar in the early morning of May 5, 1942. Their target was the huge harbor of Diego Suarez in the north of the island. A combined operation was mounted to seize the objective, with aerial support provided by aircraft from HMS *Illustrious* and HMS *Indomitable*. Within hours Diego Suarez had been taken, and by the evening of the 7th, the British were using the harbor.

The Imperial Japanese navy made only one large-scale excursion into the Indian Ocean during the Pacific War, and that was during April 1942. The Japanese fleet accounted for a number of vessels and forced Admiral Somerville's fleet to the western Indian Ocean. However, the Japanese failed to take advantage of their naval superiority. Following strikes against Ceylon and targets in the Bay of Bengal, they withdrew to the Pacific.

In September, the capital, Tananarive, fell to British forces following another amphibious operation. Any thoughts of early Vichy collapse were short-lived as pockets of resistance lasted until November 1942. However, although Japanese submarine and merchant raider activity grew briefly in the region during the mid-year months, accounting for dozens of ships, Madagascar could no longer pose a problem to the supply lines of the western Indian Ocean. Operation Ironclad had been a great success for British amphibious operations, with numerous lessons learned for use in the Mediterranean theater.

By late 1942 the Indian Ocean had become an increasingly less important theater to the war aims of the Allies. The United States had held the Japanese onslaught in the Pacific and was now building for its own offensives, while in the Atlantic and Mediterranean the Allies were preparing for Operation Torch, the invasion of North Africa. Consequently, elements of the Eastern Fleet were pulled back from the Indian Ocean for this and the later amphibious campaigns against Italy. As Correlli Barnett writes, "In the autumn the Admiralty cut the Eastern Fleet down to one carrier and two battleships, the remainder being needed in the Mediterranean to support 'Operation Torch.' In spring 1943 Somerville lost his sole remaining carrier and battleship, so reducing his fleet to cruisers and destroyers and rendering the Indian Ocean a strategic backwater."

## Dieppe

It was partly a wish to placate Soviet calls for the opening up of a second front that led to the disastrous decision to undertake the large-scale raid on the German-held port of Dieppe on August 19, 1942. Also responsible were varied political and military pressures on Churchill and his Chiefs of Staff, one of which was a wish by the latter to avoid the former forcing through an even more dangerous escapade – and the presence of Mountbatten as Chief of Combined Operations.

The Dieppe operation involved a force of 237 warships and landing craft, including eight destroyers but no battleships, which the Admiralty refused to risk. They carried almost 5,000 Canadian troops, some 1,000 British, and 50 American, and enjoyed the support of 74 squadrons from the Allied airforces. The Canadians suffered over 3,000 casualties in the operation, of whom some 900 were killed, while the British took 275 casualties and lost one destroyer, 33 landing craft, and no fewer than 106 aircraft.

## Operation Torch

The entry of the United States into the war in December 1941 completely altered the strategic situation in the Mediterranean Sea, from a desperate holding operation by the Royal Navy to an offensive theater characterized by large-scale amphibious assaults. The Allied landings in North Africa, or Operation Torch, on November 8, 1942, marked the beginning of the end for Vichy French and the German/Italian forces in North Africa.

Aptly, Admiral Cunningham was made Allied Naval Commander Expeditionary Force, although General Dwight Eisenhower was in overall command. The planning for this highly elaborate combined operation was done by the brilliant Admiral Sir Bertram Ramsay, as Deputy Naval Commander Expeditionary Force. The landings were organized in masterly fashion into the Western Assault Force (Casablanca), the Central Task Force (Oran), and the Eastern Task Force (Algiers). Just under 100,000 troops were deployed in the first phases of the operation.

The Arctic convoys were the most dangerous of all, under threat of attack by submarine, surface raider, and aircraft. Here PQ18, en route to the Soviet Union in September 1942, is seen fighting a heavy attack by the Luftwaffe. (IWM A12022)

The Allies had hoped that Tunisia would fall by February 1943, but it took the combined efforts of the Torch force and the Eighth Army from the east to bring about the surrender of the Axis forces on May 13, 1943. The Royal Navy supported not only the landings in this period but also the Eighth Army, with supplies for the Battle of El Alamein from October 23 to November 5. Allied forces sank 500 Axis merchant ships (560,000 tons) between January and May 1943 in order to cut off the enemy forces in North Africa.

## Battle of the Barents Sea

In December 1942 the Arctic convoys were resumed. The second of these, JW51B, was attacked on December 31 by the *Lützow*, the *Admiral Hipper*, and six destroyers. The Battle of the Barents Sea saw a skillful and determined defense by the convoy's destroyer escorts under Captain Robert Sherbrooke, supported by the distant cruiser escort; they forced the hesitant Germans off, for the loss of two destroyers and a minesweeper against one German destroyer. In March 1943, largely in order to divert escorts to deal with the growing menace in the Atlantic, the Arctic convoys were again discontinued.

Hitler's reaction to the failure of the attack on JW51B to achieve the expected

ABOVE German nervousness about a second front was increased by a series of British Combined Operations raids. On the night of March 27–28, 1942, HMS *Campbeltown* managed to get past the German defenses at St Nazaire and ram the dock gates, while 268 Commandos landed from smaller vessels to destroy base facilities; of 630 men involved, 144 were killed and another 200 captured. But on the following day 5 tons of explosives hidden in the *Campbeltown*'s bows exploded, putting the only dock on the Atlantic coast big enough to accommodate the German battleship *Tirpitz* out of action for the rest of the war. (IWM)

success in the Barents Sea was one of absolute fury. Admiral Dönitz replaced Raeder as Commander-in-Chief with orders to decommission the remaining major surface units and reassign their crews to the submarine service. This, in fact, did not take place, Dönitz eventually persuading a skeptical Hitler to retain them. By this time

there were some 400 operational U-boats at Dönitz's disposal, and he now had the ability to put around 100 into the Atlantic at any one time.

## Victory in the Atlantic

While, through the prodigious efforts of American shipyards in producing the prefabricated Liberty cargo vessel, the Allies could always more than replace their merchant-ship losses, the massive buildup of men and matériel that would be required for the invasion of Europe necessitated securing the Atlantic. This task was therefore given priority by the Allied Casablanca Conference in January 1943. But first the carnage in the Atlantic continued.

# Arctic convoy routes, winter and summer

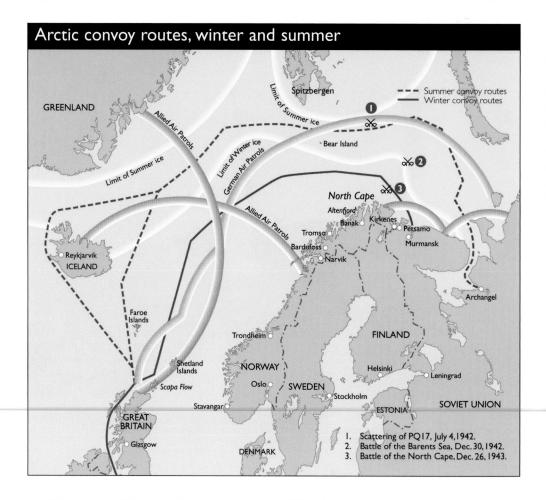

Summer convoy routes
Winter convoy routes

GREENLAND

Spitzbergen

Limit of Summer ice

Allied Air Patrols

Limit of Summer ice

Bear Island

Limit of Winter ice

German Air Patrols

**1**

**2**

**3**

North Cape

Altenfjord

Allied Air Patrols

Banak    Kirkenes

Tromsø

Petsamo

Bardufoss

Murmansk

Narvik

Reykjarvik
ICELAND

Archangel

Faroe
Islands

Trondheim

FINLAND

Shetland
Islands

NORWAY

Helsinki

Leningrad

Scapa Flow

Oslo    SWEDEN

Stavangar

Stockholm

ESTONIA

SOVIET UNION

GREAT
BRITAIN

Glasgow

DENMARK

1.  Scattering of PQ17, July 4, 1942.
2.  Battle of the Barents Sea, Dec. 30, 1942.
3.  Battle of the North Cape, Dec. 26, 1943.

ABOVE From August 1941 the Royal Navy started running vital resupply convoys around northern Norway to the beleaguered Soviet Union. Eventually, almost 4.5 million tons of war matériel would be carried by this route. But constrained by both geography and the atrocious Arctic weather and, after March 1942, subjected to the concentrated efforts of German aircraft, submarines, and surface vessels lurking in Norwegian fjords, this was the most dangerous of all convoy routes, with almost 8.5 percent of merchant vessels dispatched lost.

RIGHT Operation Ironclad was a testing ground for British amphibious operations following their initial failures earlier in the war. One area that was exploited far better than in previous landings was the use of carrier-based aircraft, particularly in larger numbers. The carriers HMS *Illustrious* and HMS *Indomitable* flew a cross section of the British naval aircraft of the time, employing Swordfish, Albacores, Fulmars, Martletts (Wildcats), and Sea Hurricanes. The *Illustrious* was also used in the successful operations in September.

If German U-boat numbers had risen, the doctrine and equipment capable of countering them had also become much improved in the previous 18 months. Great strides had been made in terms of training and tactics. There were now better and more escorts. Settled groups were formed. The ships began to receive a steady flow of new sensors and weapons. The two most important were a High Frequency Direction

Finding set (HF-DF or "Huff-Duff") and a new, revolutionary, and much more effective radar set initially operating on a wavelength of just under 4 inches (10 centimeters).

Ship-borne "Huff-Duff" exploited the U-boats' reliance on radio communications and provided instant warning of the presence of enemy submarines with sufficient accuracy to permit escorts to attack. Short-wave radar was fitted to both

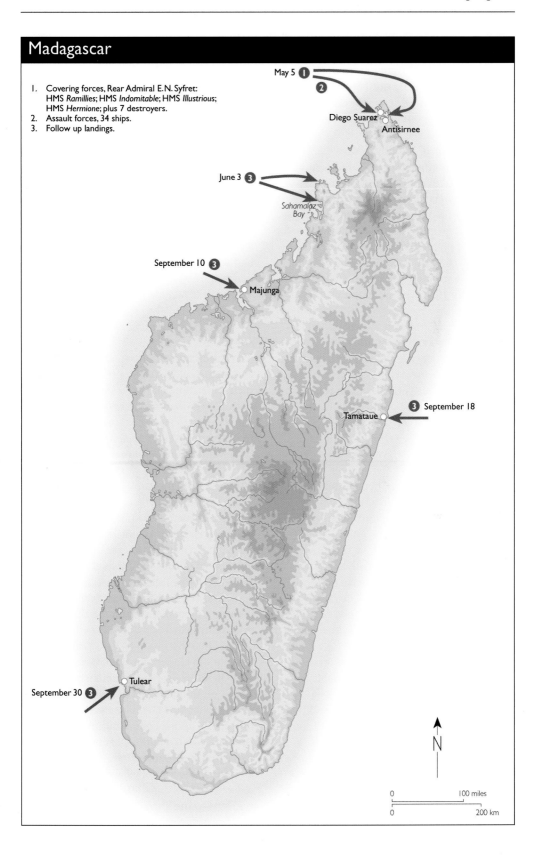

# Madagascar

1. Covering forces, Rear Admiral E.N. Syfret:
   HMS *Ramillies*; HMS *Indomitable*; HMS *Illustrious*;
   HMS *Hermione*; plus 7 destroyers.
2. Assault forces, 34 ships.
3. Follow up landings.

May 5 **1**
**2**
Diego Suarez
Antisirnee

June 3 **3**

*Sahamaloz Bay*

September 10 **3**
Majunga

**3** September 18
Tamataue

September 30 **3**
Tulear

N

| 0 | | 100 miles |
|---|---|---|
| 0 | | 200 km |

surface escorts and aircraft. U-boats were now vulnerable while they traveled on the surface. Often they would not know that they had been detected until an aircraft commenced its attack. The submarines were increasingly forced under water, where they were slow and lacked endurance.

Thus equipped, the Royal Navy's six mid-ocean groups successfully fought their fast convoys through in the autumn of 1942. However, the slow convoys were escorted by the four Canadian groups and one from the United States, which were not as well equipped. Between July and December 1942, 80 percent of mid-Atlantic losses came from Canadian-escorted convoys. By 1943 they were removed from the theater. However, the Royal Navy had sufficient escorts to form escort support groups, which could prosecute submarine contacts while leaving the convoy's own escort with the convoy.

By 1942 aircraft patrolling tactics had also become much more effective. Instead of loitering over a convoy, aircraft now operated ahead and to either side of its anticipated route, so preventing the formation of Wolf Pack patrol lines. But there was a reluctance to deploy the few very long-range (VLR) aircraft capable of covering the mid-Atlantic gap, such as the VLR Liberator. In the United States, there was an unwillingness to divert them from the Pacific; in Britain, meanwhile, throughout most of 1942 a fierce political battle was fought between the Royal Navy and Coastal Command on the one hand and Bomber Command under Air Marshal Harris on the other, over whether more long-range aircraft should be shifted from the Strategic Bombing Offensive and made available to those seeking to keep the Atlantic open. While it was eventually decided to switch aircraft to the Atlantic, it was not until the spring of 1943 that this took place. By mid-March, Coastal Command had two squadrons of B-24Ds – Liberator IIIs – the outstanding very long-range anti-submarine patrol aircraft of the war. Their arrival would be crucial.

The other method of providing air cover was to use aircraft carriers. After the costly experiments with the fleet carriers in 1939, the Admiralty explored a number of different solutions. Largely in a bid to deal with German long-range aircraft, a small number of merchant ships were at first provided with a single catapult-launched Hurricane fighter, the courageous pilot being required to bale out or ditch close to a friendly ship after his mission. More designed to counter the submarine threat and certainly for the airmen a less perilous alternative, 19 grain carriers and oil tankers had a flight deck constructed and a cramped hangar provided for four or five aircraft. While these Merchant Aircraft Carriers (MAC-ships) failed to register a U-boat kill, no convoy escorted by one suffered any losses.

An even more effective solution was the escort carrier. The Admiralty had examined such a concept before the war, and in 1941 a captured German banana boat was converted into HMS *Audacity*. During Commander Walker's defense of homeward-bound Gibraltar convoy HG76 against a large Wolf Pack in December 1941, *Audacity* had proved herself before being torpedoed. By late 1942 escort carriers built along merchant-ship lines were being mass-produced by American yards. They were put to a variety of uses, including close air support during amphibious landings. But from the spring, operated by both the Royal Navy and the US Navy, escort carriers became a permanent feature of the mid-Atlantic escort groups.

So, while the spring of 1943 initially brought only gloom for the British, matters were about to swing very rapidly in the Allies' favor. An Admiralty review later that year claimed that "the Germans never came so near to disrupting communications between the New World and the Old as in the first twenty days of March, 1943." In fact, this was an unduly pessimistic view and was more a reflection of the war-weariness of the upper echelons of the Royal Navy than an accurate analysis of the progress of the campaign.

While the losses were undoubtedly unacceptably high – more than half a million tons were lost in the first 20 days of the month – increasing numbers of convoys were being brought across without loss. In March, Bletchley Park broke back into the U-boats' Enigma traffic, from which it had been excluded for some months, but instead of being routed away from known concentrations, convoys were now being deliberately fought through in a bid to destroy the U-boats.

By April the total number of U-boats in the North Atlantic reached its maximum of 101, formed into four huge packs. But the advantage increasingly lay with the Allies. For example, the unladen westbound convoy ONS5 was repeatedly attacked during May 4 and 5 by no fewer than 41 U-boats of the Wolf Pack Group Fink. The convoy lost 12 merchant ships, but seven of the attackers were destroyed, another five were damaged, and two more were lost to a collision, forcing U-boat Command to call off that attack.

The German losses continued. During May 41 U-boats were lost. By the month's end, Dönitz had recalled his packs. They could no longer operate on the surface or penetrate the escort screens. The U-boats had to regroup and devise another strategy and wait for new equipment. Fortunately for the Allies, that new equipment would not be available in sufficient numbers before the end of the war. The Atlantic was now effectively secure from submarines in readiness for the buildup for Operation Overlord and the invasion of Europe.

## Operation Husky

Operation Husky, or the invasion of Sicily on July 10, 1943, marked a new chapter in the battle for the Mediterranean Sea. Approximately 2,590 warships and landing craft were used to land around 80,000 troops (450,000 eventually), 300 tanks, and 7,000 mechanized vehicles (the majority British) in Italian territory over a three-day period. The amphibious assaults on the southern part of the island went well due to the careful planning of Ramsay and the weight of naval fire support: six battleships, 10 cruisers, and a multitude of destroyers as well as two aircraft carriers.

Despite putting up fierce resistance, the Italian and German troops were forced to withdraw back to the Italian mainland between August 11 and 16. The extraction of these troops was a remarkable feat stemming from the excellent planning of Admiral Barone (Italian navy) and Captain von Liebenstein (German navy), saving approximately 117,000 troops in a classic amphibious withdrawal. The significance of Husky was underscored by the collapse of the Mussolini government on July 25, and on September 8 the new Italian government accepted an armistice that led to the surrender of the Italian fleet a day later.

At the same time, Operation Avalanche was initiated, with large-scale landings on the Italian mainland at Salerno Bay. The landing forces comprised 27 battalions of infantry with 150 tanks and nearly 350 pieces of artillery, supported by two brigades of Commandos and US Rangers. The fight was slow and extremely painful for the Allies in the face of excellent German defensive tactics. The formidable Gustav Line forced the Allies to make another amphibious landing at Anzio on January 22, 1944. Rome finally fell on June 6, 1944, the same day that the second front was opened in France with Operation Overlord.

## The end of the war in the Mediterranean

The Mediterranean campaign ended in disappointment for the Allies, who did not manage to eject Field Marshal Kesselring's formidable Army Group C from Italy until April 1945, by which time the war was virtually over. For Britain the Mediterranean offered, in the early stages of the war, the

# The Atlantic

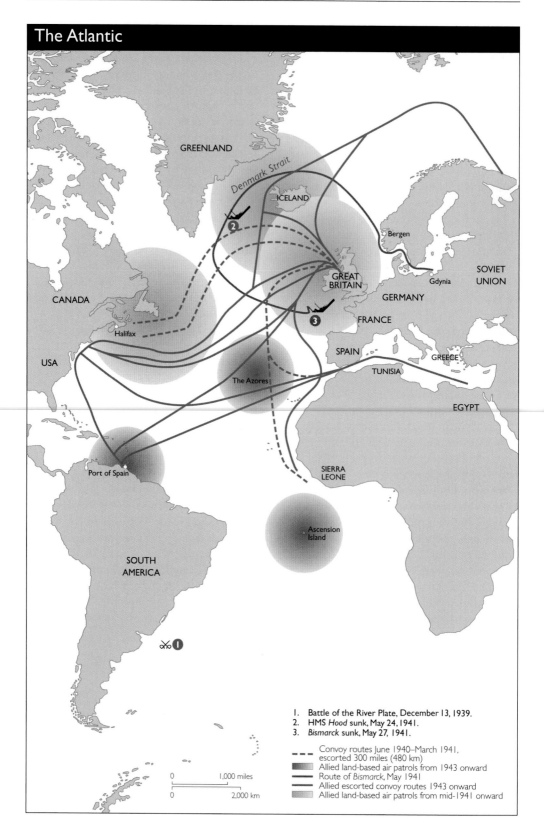

GREENLAND

Denmark Strait

ICELAND

Bergen

② ✕

GREAT
BRITAIN

Gdynia

SOVIET
UNION

CANADA

GERMANY

③ ✕

Halifax

FRANCE

USA

SPAIN

GREECE

TUNISIA

The Azores

EGYPT

Port of Spain

SIERRA
LEONE

SOUTH
AMERICA

Ascension
Island

✄❶

1.    Battle of the River Plate, December 13, 1939.
2.    HMS *Hood* sunk, May 24, 1941.
3.    *Bismarck* sunk, May 27, 1941.

- - -     Convoy routes June 1940–March 1941,
            escorted 300 miles (480 km)
▓▓      Allied land-based air patrols from 1943 onward
━━━     Route of *Bismarck*, May 1941
━━━     Allied escorted convoy routes 1943 onward
▓▓      Allied land-based air patrols from mid-1941 onward

| 0 | | 1,000 miles |
|---|---|---|
| 0 | | 2,000 km |

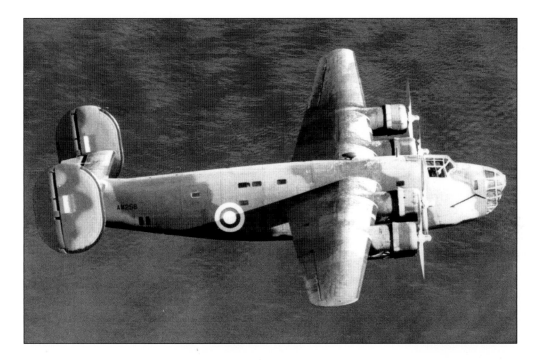

ABOVE German U-boats relied on moving on the surface. Maritime air power, especially when equipped with radar, denied them this essential freedom of maneuver. The versatile and very long-range US Liberator, seen here in a transport version, was essential in closing the mid-Atlantic gap in the spring of 1943. (Topham Picturepoint)

LEFT The key to the naval war was control of the Atlantic. Forays of large German surface units such as Bismarcks could be dealt with. However, continuing the menace of German submarine Wolf Packs that preyed on Allied convoy routes, which grew in complexity as the war progressed, was a much greater problem. It was not until the late spring of 1943 that adequate control of the Atlantic had been acquired with the increasing availability of very long-range land-based maritime patrol aircraft playing a vital role.

only means by which its land forces could successfully engage the Axis forces, but even that effort was protracted and drawn out. All of these military operations were totally dependent on a highly stretched Royal Navy to maintain the vital supply links with the home base. It did so with few resources, great courage, and inspired leadership from commanders such as Cunningham and Somerville.

Germany perceived the North Africa campaign and, for that matter, the subsequent Italian front as purely diversionary theaters in which its military leaders, Rommel and Kesselring, excelled. As for the Americans, they were reluctantly tied into the Mediterranean campaign by their British allies, who realized that the United States' desire to open up a second front in France before 1944 would have been disastrous. In sum, the Mediterranean theater brought about the collapse of Hitler's major ally in Europe, Italy, and provided critical experience in combined operations before the all-important invasion of France in June 1944.

## Tirpitz and Scharnhorst

Despite the 1943 victory over the Wolf Packs in the Atlantic, there still existed a threat from the remaining German heavy surface units, the Tirpitz and the Scharnhorst. By May 1943 both of these powerful vessels were lurking in the fjords of northern Norway. Their presence tied down a large British force and not only posed a threat to Atlantic shipping but also had the potential to disrupt the Overlord landings. In

Envisaged by prewar planners, it was not until late 1942 that escort carriers built on merchant ship lines were being mass-produced by US yards. They were used for a variety of purposes, including close air support during amphibious landings. But from the spring of 1943, operated by both the Royal Navy and the US Navy, escort carriers became a permanent feature of the mid-Atlantic escort groups. Here HMS *Emperor* is seen in the middle of an Atlantic gale in 1944. (IWM A24181)

September 1943, Royal Navy X-craft – midget submarines – managed to break through the *Tirpitz*'s defenses in Altenfjord and mine her, putting her out of action for six months.

In order to deal with the crisis in the Atlantic, convoys to Russia had been suspended at the beginning of 1943. Their resumption in December 1943 and the worsening situation for Germany on the Eastern Front led Admiral Dönitz to order their interception with his last operational capital ship, the *Scharnhorst*. However, these convoys were also the bait that Admiral

Bruce Fraser, Commander-in-Chief of the British Home Fleet, used to set a trap. Forewarned by Bletchley Park, Fraser mounted a skillful operation in which the German vessel, under Admiral Erich Bey, was caught between Fraser's two squadrons in appalling conditions off the northern Cape on December 26, and was sunk with the loss of 2,000 of her crew.

There remained the *Tirpitz*. In April 1944, Fraser's Home Fleet launched Operation Tungsten, in which no fewer than six British carriers launched two successful air strikes against the German ship, seriously damaging her. These were among 22 air strikes launched against the vessel. On November 12, 1944, relegated to being used as a floating artillery battery at Tromso, *Tirpitz* was hit by at least two 12,000 lb Tallboy bombs dropped by RAF Lancasters. She capsized with the loss of some 1,000 lives.

## Operation Overlord

Victory against the Germans required a major landing in northwest Europe. After considerable deliberation, the British and Americans agreed to such an operation at the Casablanca conference in January 1943. Planning and preparation began for what became the largest and most complex amphibious operation in military history, with the initial plan being approved by the Quebec conference in August 1943.

As a result of an extensive intelligence appraisal of possible landing areas, it was decided to land on the Calvados coast of Normandy between Le Havre and the Cherbourg peninsula, rather than at the more heavily defended area around Calais. However, through a complex and successful strategic deception program, the Germans were led to believe that the landings would take place at Calais. To overcome the lack of a deep-water port in the landing zone, two huge prefabricated harbors (Mulberries) were constructed in Britain to be towed across the Channel and assembled off the invasion coast.

Responsibility for the naval and amphibious operations – code-named Operation Neptune – was given to Admiral Sir Bertram Ramsay, acting under the Allied Supreme Commander, General Dwight D. Eisenhower. By the beginning of June, in the immediate area the Kriegsmarine had at its disposal a force of 25 U-boats, five destroyers, and 39 E-boats. To protect the landings, the Allies assembled a force of 286 destroyers, sloops, frigates, corvettes, and trawlers, almost 80 percent of which were provided by the Royal Navy. Six support groups, including the escort carriers *Activity*, *Tracker,* and *Vindex*, formed a screen to cover the Western Approaches and the Bay of Biscay, while the other end of the Channel was covered by another four groups. RAF Coastal Command flew extensive patrols over all support groups.

To sweep five safe passages through the mid-Channel minefields, a force of 287 minesweepers of various kinds was brought together. The D-Day landings themselves were undertaken by a force of 1,213 warships, including no fewer than seven battleships, two monitors, 23 cruisers, 100 destroyers, 130 frigates and corvettes, and over 4,000 landing ships and craft, many of specialist design. The majority of the warships were British. Some of the landing craft had been converted to fire thousands of rockets to provide additional naval fire support for the assault and to help overcome the extensive German Atlantic Wall defenses.

These assault elements were divided into two forces. The Eastern Task Force under Rear Admiral Sir Philip Vian was responsible for landing the 2nd British Army of British and Canadian troops on the Gold, Juno, and Sword beaches between the River Orne and Port-en-Bessin. The Western Task Force under the American Rear Admiral Alan G. Kirk was responsible for landing the 1st US Army on Omaha and Utah beaches between Port-en-Bessin and Varreville. By the beginning of June 1944 the ports and estuaries of Britain were packed with warships and transports of all kinds as the Allied Expeditionary Force was engaged.

By the summer of 1944, partly as a by-product of the Strategic Bombing Offensive, the Allies had effectively

destroyed the Luftwaffe in the west. Before the landings, the beachhead had been largely cut off from the rest of France by the systematic wrecking of the French transportation system from the air. Any attempts by the Germans to reinforce their coastal forces would be hit by roaming Allied fighter-bombers. The landings were conducted with the enormous benefit of not just air superiority but air supremacy. Over 14,000 air sorties were flown on the first day.

After a day's delay because of poor weather, Operation Neptune began just after midnight on June 6, 1944 – D-Day – with Allied airborne landings aimed at securing the flanks of the invasion area. With heavy naval gunfire support, the first troops began going ashore in the American sector on the Utah and Omaha beaches at 6:30 am, with British and Canadian troops going ashore an hour

ABOVE The King George V-class battleship *Duke of York*. Serving as Admiral Sir Bruce Fraser's flagship in December 1943, she took part in the trapping and destruction of the German battlecruiser *Scharnhorst*. While the Royal Navy has been criticized for a prewar overemphasis on these leviathans of the seas, it was their possession that prevented German vessels such as the *Scharnhorst* and the even more capable *Bismarck* and *Tirpitz* running amok among the transatlantic convoys. (IWM A7552)

RIGHT Admiral Sir Bertram Ramsay was one of a number of outstanding senior British naval officers during World War II. He came to dominate Allied amphibious operations in the European theater through his masterminding of the Dunkirk evacuation and his involvement with the planning and conduct of the Allied landings in North Africa and Sicily in 1942 and 1943. He was also the meticulous Naval Commander-in-Chief for the Normandy landings in 1944. (IWM A23443)

later on Gold, Juno, and Sword. By the end of D-Day, 57,500 American troops and 75,215 British and Canadian troops had

LEFT, TOP An integral part of the success of the Overlord landings was the use of naval gunfire support undertaken by seven battleships, 23 cruisers, 100 destroyers, and 130 frigates and corvettes, mostly provided by the Royal Navy. Here HMS *Warspite's* 15-inch (381 mm) guns are seen engaging German fortifications on the Calvados coast. (IWM A23914)

LEFT, BOTTOM Testimony to the huge logistical scale of the Normandy landings is this scene on Omaha beach, with scores more vessels waiting offshore. (IWM EA26941)

BELOW Larger and faster aircraft such as Seafires and Hellcats (pictured below) encountered serious landing problems when operating off smaller carriers such as the Escort Carriers (CVEs) of the East Indian Fleet. However, their speed and firepower were crucial for achieving successful missions against the Japanese. (IWM)

been landed. When the assault phase – Operation Neptune – concluded officially at the end of the month, 850,279 men, 148,803 vehicles, and 570,505 tons of supplies had been brought ashore.

Following the Allies' breakout from the Normandy beachhead, their armies continued to receive naval support as they moved up the coast of Europe. The Kriegsmarine tried to disrupt these operations by unleashing midget submarines from bases in Holland. Conventional U-boats had also begun to operate in shallower water around the British Isles, but the shallow water played havoc with the asdic (sonar) sets and the proximity of land

## Normandy landings

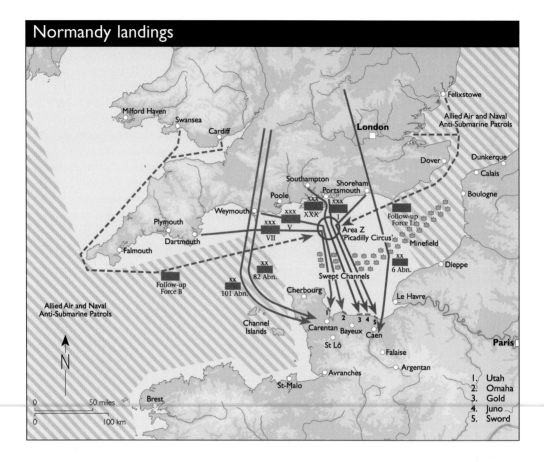

Felixstowe

Milford Haven
Swansea
Cardiff

London

Allied Air and Naval
Anti-Submarine Patrols

Dover
Dunkerque
Calais

Southampton    Shoreham
Portsmouth
Poole
Boulogne

Weymouth
Plymouth    XXX    XXX    XXX
I
Follow-up
Force L
Area Z
'Picadilly Circus'
Minefield

Dartmouth    V
VII
Falmouth

XX
6 Abn.
Dieppe

XX
82 Abn.    Swept Channels

Follow-up
Force B    XX
101 Abn.    Cherbourg    Le Havre

Allied Air and Naval
Anti-Submarine Patrols

Channel
Islands    1  2  3 4 5
Carentan  Bayeux  Caen
St Lô    Falaise

N    Avranches    Argentan

Paris

St-Malo    1. Utah
2. Omaha
3. Gold
4. Juno
5. Sword

0    50 miles
Brest
0    100 km

adversely affected other sensors such
as radar.

The "death-ride of the U-boats"
nevertheless continued: no fewer than
151 U-boats were lost to Allied action in
1945, for the loss of only 46 Allied
merchantmen, a fraction of the 1942 rate
of destruction. The U-boat arm had begun
to receive submarines equipped with a
Schnorchel device that allowed submarines
to recharge their batteries without exposing
more than the top of the breathing device,
and even more worrying for the Allies,
high-speed Type XXI and Type XXIII
submarines were introduced against which
the slower escorts had little answer.
Fortunately for the Allied naval effort,
however, the Germans were not able to
produce these in sufficient quantity by the
time the yards building them – subjected to
increasingly heavy and accurate air attack –
had been overrun in 1945.

D-Day saw US and British airborne landings on either
flank of the assault areas to protect the Allied seaborne
landings. Forces arrived in Area Z from the southern half
of Great Britain - follow-up forces would come from the
whole country - and several thousand vessels of all kinds
were funnelled through narrow channels that had been
cleared of deep-water mines. By the end of June 6
57,500 American and 75,215 British and Canadian
troops would be ashore.

## Victory in the Indian Ocean

As the naval war began to decrease in
intensity in the European theater following
Operation Overlord in June 1944, the Royal
Navy and Churchill transferred their naval
attention – though not necessarily at the
same speed – to the Indian and Pacific
oceans. Initially, the Indian Ocean, with the
continuing land campaign in Burma, was
seen as a priority, for it was felt, politically,
that the lost territories must be retaken.

## D-Day gun duels

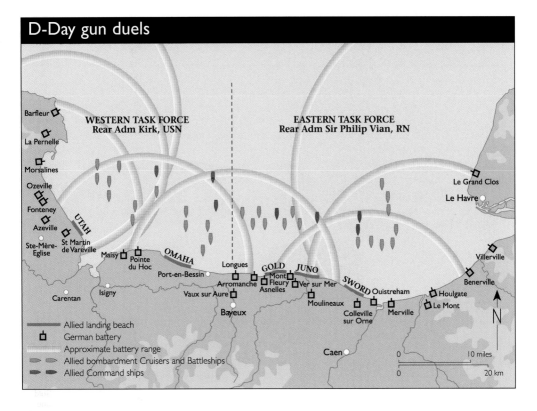

**WESTERN TASK FORCE**
Rear Adm Kirk, USN

**EASTERN TASK FORCE**
Rear Adm Sir Philip Vian, RN

Barfleur
La Pernelle
Morsalines
Ozeville
Fonteney
Azeville
Ste-Mère-Eglise    St Martin de Vareville    UTAH
Maisy    Pointe du Hoc    OMAHA    Longues    GOLD    JUNO
Port-en-Bessin    Mont    SWORD
Arromanche    Fleury    Ver sur Mer    Ouistreham
Carentan    Isigny    Asnelles    Houlgate
Vaux sur Aure    Moulineaux    Merville    Le Mont
Bayeux    Colleville sur Orne
Le Grand Clos
Le Havre
Villerville
Benerville
Caen

━━━ Allied landing beach
⌂ German battery
Approximate battery range
◖▶ ◖▶ Allied bombardment Cruisers and Battleships
◖▶ ◖▶ Allied Command ships

0        10 miles
0        20 km

N

There were also the benefits of massive production coming through to the Indian Ocean as large numbers of escort carriers and much more capable carrier aircraft entered service – the very equipment that Admiral Somerville had wanted for the Eastern Fleet in 1942.

The Eastern Fleet, however, had been essentially defensive in outlook, acting as a fleet-in-being, deterring Japanese incursions into the Indian Ocean and safeguarding the vital convoy routes. The new fleets that were to become active for 1945, the East Indies Fleet and the British Pacific Fleet, were very much offensively oriented. The role of the East Indies Fleet was to support the British Fourteenth Army as it pushed the Japanese back through Burma using escort carriers, escorts including battleships and cruisers, and a large amphibious force. It was also there to neutralize the Japanese warships in the region and stop them from entering the Indian Ocean. In addition, it was tasked to destroy the remaining Japanese land-based air units in the theater.

In an attempt to protect the coast German forces had created an Atlantic Wall of mines, obstacles, and gun emplacements. While not as formidably defended as some sections of the coast, the German heavy gun batteries in Normandy were sited to cover the entire landing area with interlocking arcs of fire, and unmolested would have made the landings impossible. An essential feature that made the Allied landings possible was the presence of large numbers of heavy naval vessels to counter the threat posed by these guns.

Through a series of amphibious raids and assaults, offensive carrier fighter missions and the sinking of the Japanese heavy cruiser *Haguro*, these aims were successfully achieved, so much so that by May the land-based Japanese air and sea forces no longer posed a threat. By this point the East Indies Fleet was a substantial force, employing two battleships, nine escort carriers, two ferry carriers, and dozens of cruisers, destroyers, submarines, and amphibious warfare vessels. It was a force far removed from the earlier Eastern Fleet, and one that could finally engage the Japanese on superior terms. The fleet remained in the

The combination of the American advance in the Pacific and the British advances in Burma and the Indian Ocean saw a collapse in the Japanese ability to defend against amphibious operations in the Bay of Bengal by 1945. Here British forces are approaching Rangoon. The Japanese had already withdrawn. Note the landing craft, far removed from the very early operations of 1940. (IWM IND4659)

Indian Ocean supporting the land campaign and Japan's withdrawal from the region until the defeat of the Japanese Empire.

It can be argued that the Eastern Fleet was overshadowed by its much larger sister fleet, the British Pacific Fleet: not only in terms of firepower and size, but also by the fact that the Pacific Fleet was engaged in the heart of the Japanese Empire and against the last remaining substantial Japanese assets. Either way, the formation and employment of the British Pacific Fleet in early 1945 signaled the end of the Indian Ocean as a major theater of operations.

# Peter Herbert Owen, Royal Navy midshipman

When the naval war came, it brought a harshness and violence that had not been expected. For most naval personnel it also brought a very steep learning curve, as many of them had never seen conflict before. Much of the interwar period had been spent on training cruises, goodwill visits, and tours. The younger members of ships' companies were uninitiated in the ways of war and had only experienced them through their elders and reading the histories and memoirs of the First World War and before.

This was especially true of the naval officer cadets of Britain. One such young man was Midshipman Peter Herbert Owen, who joined the battleship HMS *Royal Oak* in August 1939 having graduated from Dartmouth Naval College at the start of May. Owen had spent four years in the College, starting as a boy cadet in 1935. During his four years' training in Dartmouth, he had undertaken various naval and academic courses, and taken part in numerous sports. Soon, however, he and his classmates would come to the end of their summer cruises. They would become embroiled in events and adventures that they had sought from the start of their young naval careers, but for which their training could never have adequately prepared them. Yet during the war and through all of their experiences they evolved and matured, and with the mass input of wartime reservist and volunteer reservist officers, formed the backbone of the junior officer corps of the Royal Navy.

Owen was no exception. His reporting of the war in his midshipman's journal during its first two years begins to take on a hardened and matter-of-fact edge within a month of the hostilities breaking out, with his account of the sinking of HMS *Royal Oak* in October 1939. Owen, upon being sent to his ship, was tasked with keeping a journal for the remainder of his time at sea as a midshipman – in his case, almost two years. Officers supervising midshipmen were to ensure that the journals demonstrated powers of observation, expression, and orderliness.

At the start of hostilities in the late summer of 1939, the British Home Fleet had moved to Scapa Flow, its war station in the Orkneys, a repeat of the Grand Fleet's action during the Great War. But like the move, the defenses of 1939 were the same as in 1914–18, with very little having been done to modernize them. Time and weathering had taken their toll on the blockships defending the anchorage, and a gap had developed between the defenses that were used to protect Kirk Sound, the entrance to Scapa. The Germans, through aerial reconnaissance, had detected this gap and Admiral Dönitz, Commander-in-Chief of the U-boats, started planning a daring strike against the superior capital ship fleet of the Royal Navy.

On the night of October 13–14, 1939, a German submarine, *U-47*, commanded by Lt Gunther Prien, successfully penetrated the defenses of the British naval base and sank the *Royal Oak* with four torpedoes. Prien's first salvo seemed ineffective, but his second found the desired target, ironically the only capital ship in Scapa at the time.

Owen, who was a midshipman on board, expands upon this loss in graphic detail:

*It was at about 0120 on the morning of Saturday, October 14, when the ship was lying in berth B12 in Scapa Flow, that the tremendous explosion woke up the ship's company. The general assumption was that a bomb had hit us and many men manned their AA stations; others went under armor; but very many turned over and went to sleep again. The Captain*

*immediately went for'ard to locate the trouble and was soon joined by the Commander and Engineer Commander, who proceeded to flood the inflammable store and smell the escaping gases. Meanwhile the magazine temperatures were taken, and almost everyone turned in again assuming that the Captain had rectified the trouble – whatever it might be!*

*It must have been about 0130 when the Admiral crossed the Quarter Deck on his way for'ard and gave the only order of the evening – "drifter raise steam at once." At the same time*

Britannia Royal Naval College, Dartmouth, was designed to give young cadets a safe and steady introduction to the navy. The cadets' training evolved from the middle part of the nineteenth century, when the college was on a pair of hulks in the river, to a purpose-built college in the first decade of the twentieth century, taking into account the steam and machine age. Their instruction and education was in the hands of a mixture of naval officers and civilian masters. (National Maritime Museum)

*the W/T (water tight) door Lieutenant went off on his rounds as all the doors were open and the hatches were all suspended on their Weston*

The *Royal Oak* was the most modern of the "R"-class battleships, having been partly modified during the interwar period. However, her subdivisions and watertight integrity were totally overwhelmed by Prien's attack. It was particularly sobering to note that the rest of the fleet was not in Scapa Flow at the time. The loss was a major blow to the Royal Navy, following so soon after the loss of HMS *Courageous* to submarine attack in September. (IWM Q65784)

*purchases. The midshipmen had just been shaken by the instructor Lieutenant when at 0140 three, or possibly four, shattering explosions occurred at about three-second intervals and the ship immediately started listing to starboard.*

*When this happened the senior officers were still smelling gases in the cable locker, and they apparently did not realize that the smell had been made by the cable running out after the first explosion; the sparks from the cable passing around the cable-holder and a cloud of spray the only external signs noted by the look-outs in the ADP, who were still placidly looking for aircraft.*

*And so twenty minutes after the ship had first been torpedoed no definite steps had been taken by anyone to save the ship or her company, and there was no more time as the final explosions had caused her to heel over very rapidly – she was keel uppermost seven minutes later, according to witnesses in the Pegasus.*

*As the ship started listing the lights went out, and the ladders grew progressively more difficult*

*for even one man to negotiate – and virtually impossible for the 1100-odd men trapped below. Several sliding hatches on the port side slid shut, and many Weston purchases snapped from sheer weight of men hauling themselves up, so that the boys and stokers and topmen had little chance of escape. Of one hundred and fifty Royal Marines only fifty managed to escape, many of them coming through scuttles.*

*The boats were all lashed down except the PB and launch at the starboard booms and the gig on the Quarter Deck. The picket boat got away and picked up about sixty men and all went well until the officer in charge told these men to paddle, causing the boat to roll over on her beams and shaking off several people, who finally capsized the outfight by trying to climb back; it was never possible to flash up the boiler. The only man to reach the launch at the boom was the midshipman of the boat, who unfortunately was not able to clear her before she was pulled under as she was moored up by too short a strap. The gig was on the Quarter Deck and the combined efforts of most of the officers was insufficient to launch her; she floated off upside down.*

*The drifter Daisy D was alongside abreast P.6 gun and the skipper held on until she was partially lifted out of the water by the bilge, in order that as many people as possible might jump aboard – an opportunity of which only one*

Prien (shown above with his wife) was welcomed home to national acclaim following his sinking of the *Royal Oak*, one of the first for Germany. He and the other successful U-boat commanders soon became national heroes. However, gradually they were either captured or killed. (IWM HU40836)

*midshipman in mess kit availed himself. The skipper was awarded the DSC for hazarding his ship. Many of the carley floats had been damaged by heavy seas and the rest were lashed down; only the Commander thought to free any of these.*

## H.M.S. "Royal Sovereign's" Routes.

| DATE | | | |
|---|---|---|---|
| January 15th | 1940 | | Left Spithead |
| " 23 | " | | Arrived Halifax. N.S.  Convoy duties. |
| April 10 | " | | Left Halifax |
| " 23 | " | | Arrived Gibraltar |
| " 28 | " | | Left   Gibraltar |
| May 3 | " | | Arrived Alexandria . |
| | | | Worked with mediterranean Fleet |
| August 11 | " | | Left Alexandria . through Suez |
| " 16 | " | | Arrived Aden |
| " 29 | " | | Left Aden |
| Sept 15 | " | | Arrived Durban Dry Dock |
| October 5 | " | | Alongside at Durban |
| " 23 | " | | Left Durban |
| " 26 | " | | Arrived & left Capetown. |
| November 4 | " | | Arrived Freetown. (Out & in once). |
| " 10 | " | | Left Freetown . |
| November 18 | 1940 | | Arrived Gibraltar again |
| December 1 | " | | Left Gibraltar |
| December 10 | " | | Returned Halifax & convoy duties |
| March 4 | 1941 | | Arrived Bermuda for leave & |
| " 7 | " | | Left Bermuda . (Recreation !! |

*COMMANDING OFFICER*
*20 MAR 1941*
*H.M.S. "ROYAL SOVEREIGN"*

In the water there must have been about six hundred men, of whom very many were picked up by the drifter off the port quarter and beam. Others met their fate with the PB and quite a number were picked up by boats from the Pegasus; fifteen men reached the shore and the remaining two hundred were drowned. The Flow was extremely cold and there was very little

The last journal entry of Owen as a midshipman. It demonstrates the almost continuous use of the naval assets of Britain. More importantly, it shows the geographical range and scope of operations of the *Royal Sovereign*. (BRNC)

wreckage about; on the starboard side the oil fuel was very oppressive indeed, and many men brought up solid oil for hours afterwards.

*Apart from these 15 men who went to Kirkwall, all the survivors were taken on board the* Pegasus *and sent into the engine-room to thaw. No one was disturbed until they were transferred to the depot ship* Voltaire *at about 0900 on Saturday where they remained till Tuesday.*

The Royal Navy lost over 800 officers and men with the sinking of the *Royal Oak*. Her sinking in a British anchorage led to the safety of Scapa and the Home Fleet being seriously questioned. Thus, following the sinking, the rest of the Home Fleet was dispersed to ports around Scotland. This initially caused a weakening in the ability of the Royal Navy to blockade the German surface fleet; however, the much smaller German navy was unable to exploit this physically minor but huge propaganda coup with any other tangible results following their initial strike. The defenses around Scapa Flow were strengthened, eventually incorporating a causeway across Kirk Sound and Water Sound known as "Churchill's Barrier."

The Home Fleet soon returned to Scapa and remained based there, in safety, until the end of the war. As for the Captain of *U-47*, Gunther Prien, he and all his crew would be killed in action in March 1941. But for Owen it wasn't the end of the tragic episode. While he was on board the *Voltaire*, the Luftwaffe attacked the anchorage early on the Tuesday of transfer.

*We had no guns to man and so everyone leaned through the scuttles and watched four German planes as they dived over the* Iron Duke *– I actually saw the two bombs, dropped from about 150', which burst just alongside this old battleship causing her to list heavily to starboard*

*so that she was only saved by being pushed on the mud by about fifteen trawlers.*

Following this the survivors from the *Royal Oak* were taken ashore for safety; they endured another air raid at 3:00 pm the same afternoon, but with little damage. Owen writes: "The only humorous side of it was the view of four hundred 'Royal Oaks' in vests, pants and boiler suits, clutching the earth … with bombs whining all round them." That evening they were to go on leave.

In January 1940, Owen was posted to a sister ship of the *Royal Oak* when he joined HMS *Royal Sovereign*. From there his next 14 months were ones of constant activity. He was in the thick of momentous times and operations, particularly convoy work in the Atlantic, Mediterranean, and Indian oceans. Once, escorting merchant ships to Malta, he found himself "in sight of Crete nearly all of Monday and colossal bombing raids took place" against his convoy. Even more amazing for him was the sight of French ships in Alexandria harbor being rendered incapable by Admiral Cunningham's Mediterranean Fleet. "At the beginning of July it became obvious that effective measures had to be taken to prevent the French fleet falling into enemy hands. As we could not afford the ships to blockade them in port it was necessary to demobilize them."

Owen spent the remainder of his time plying the vital convoy routes, deterring attack from German surface raiders. After almost two years as a midshipman he became a sublieutenant in 1941 and a full lieutenant two years later, serving with HMS *Fernie* and then HMS *Eaglet* for the Commander-in-Chief Western Approaches. When he became a sublieutenant, his journal came to an end.

# The impact of war

World War II had a profound impact on global affairs, touching virtually every continent in the world and generating violence on an unprecedented scale. Some estimates of the total number of dead attributable to this conflict suggest that perhaps 30 million people died across the world – about three times the number of World War I. The political map of Europe was dramatically altered during this period; nations were subjugated, crushed, or simply destroyed. Famous cities like London, Berlin, and Moscow, renowned for their cultural activities, now became military targets for intensive bomber operations, appearing to bomber crews as glowing smudges of light beneath darkened bombsights. The civilian as much as the soldier was a legitimate target. Ethnic affiliation was a matter of life or death in some countries, and millions were slaughtered in the pursuit of racial purity. On the front lines, survival was a highly relative concept and people lived from day to day, with little regard for the future.

Such were the demands of total war, in which all aspects of society played a part in victory or surrender. Looking through the filter of the horrifying postwar imagery of World War II, such as the Blitz and the Holocaust, it is easy to forget that life still went on as usual. People got married, babies were born, and the elderly still existed. Not everyone was a combat soldier, sailor, or airman, and indeed the sharp end of society could not function effectively without the vital contribution of the civilians. Several historians have labelled World War II the "People's War."

## Great Britain

In Britain, the nation that declared war first, the period 1939–45 produced some remarkable political, economic, and social consequences. A new leader emerged in 1940, the arch military interventionist, Winston Churchill. His interventions were often disastrous, but he was the man of the moment and millions of people tuned into his radio broadcasts, which kept the nation's morale high. A

*The strategic bomber offensive*

The strategic bomber offensive was perceived in the 1930s as the miracle cure to avoid fighting in trenches and prolonged war. The idea, put forward by an Italian air power theorist, Giulio Douhet, in his book *The Command of the Air* (1927) was that a bombing campaign could tear out the guts of a nation, physically and psychologically, without the need to adopt the traditional and costly method of defeating armies in the field. These notions were taken up by the highly influential Chief of the Royal Air Force, Air Marshal Lord Trenchard, and implemented by the commander of Bomber Command, Air Marshal Arthur Harris, during the war.

The results of Britain's bomber offensive in Germany were highly controversial: first, it took three years of war before the RAF had the right equipment, such as Lancaster bombers, or the number of aircraft to create significant damage; and secondly, studies suggest that bombing merely reinforced morale rather than destroying it. The use of the atomic bomb on Japan in August 1945 is used as the ultimate vindication for the strategy, but question marks still remain as to whether strategic bombing could bring about the defeat of a nation without recourse to armies and navies.

Winston Churchill was the most flamboyant of all the wartime leaders. His speeches were rousing and pugnacious, typifying the bulldog spirit of a besieged Britain. In military terms, Churchill, despite his ancestral link to the great General Marlborough, was no strategist and his meddling in military affairs led to the disaster in Norway in 1940 and the abortive intervention in Greece in 1941, which prolonged the North African campaign by an additional two years; he also ordered troops into Singapore at the moment of its collapse. Luckily for Britain, he possessed one of the most able military advisers that the nation has ever produced in the form of Field Marshal Alan Brooke, who managed to offset and temper some of his more reckless ideas. (IWM HU62981)

*Rationing*

It was inevitable that food would have to be rationed in Britain given that the country, prior to the outbreak of war, depended on imports for two-thirds of its food supply. Every man, woman, and child received a ration book. An adult ration book lasted for 26 weeks and devoted five out of the 12 pages to the major food commodities, one page each for bacon or ham, margarine or butter, and lard, plus two for meat. Even clothes and gasoline were rationed, such was the dire state of the supply line to Britain. Rationing continued for many years after World War II, with meat finally being de-rationed in 1954.

*The Royal Family*

The Royal Family played an important part in keeping the national spirit going. On the eve of the anticipated invasion of Britain (Operation Sea Lion), the King, George VI, was to be found practicing his pistol shooting in the grounds of Buckingham Palace, making his intentions quite clear. The palace also sustained some bomb damage during the war, which led the Queen to state that she could now look in the eye of those living in the heavily bombed East End of London.

government of national unity was formed and the home front became the responsibility of the Labor Party under Clement Attlee. The seeds of national insurance, the welfare state, and the National Health Service were sown in this period. Economically, the cost of the war was ruinous. One estimate places the price (in today's figures) at around 940 billion U.S. dollars (£600 billion).

On a social level, everything changed. The wide-scale introduction of women into the British workforce, 3 million more in 1943 than in 1939, altered the relationship between the genders and also affected social aspirations. More people went out to eat, which was reflected in increased production from 79 million meals in 1941 to 170 million meals in 1944. Sexual relations were also liberated; people lived for the moment. Food was rationed but, ironically, the health of the nation improved, especially that of the poor.

The widespread bombing of Britain by the Luftwaffe produced two effects: first, the evacuation of just under 2 million women and children brought town and countryside together on a large scale, with a broadening of vistas on both sides; secondly, the myth of the psychological "knock-out" blow was exploded. Strategic bombing merely reinforced the morale of major cities such as

London, despite its suffering 51,509 civilians killed. The cinema became one of the most popular social recreations of the war (the high point of the British film industry) and also one of the best means of transmitting government propaganda to the people.

## Continental Europe

In Europe, life was radically transformed in some countries. In France, the armistice produced a bizarre situation. German troops were in Paris (so too was Hitler at one stage, on a visit), but the rest of the country settled down to accepting the occupation and the semiliberated existence in Vichy France under Marshal Pétain. In many ways, the

In 1944, offensives by the Red Army were organized on a massive scale. Operation Bagration from June 22, 1944, against the German army, specifically Army Group Center, in White Russia involved 2,715 tanks and 1,355 self-propelled artillery. In just one week, 130,000 enemy troops were captured and 900 tanks destroyed. Within two months of this offensive, the German army had lost close to 300,000 men and the Red Army had moved forward by 350 miles (560 km). (IWM NYP72428)

*The Special Operations Executive*
The SOE was another of Churchill's ideas to create discontent in occupied Europe. In July 1940, he ordered Hugh Dalton, the Minister for Economic Warfare, "to set Europe ablaze" and this unit was aimed primarily at subverting the activities of the German forces on the continent. SOE agents, both men and women, were parachuted into Europe to provide intelligence, set up resistance movements, and sabotage the Nazi war effort. This highly secret organization was remarkably successful.

reaction of the average French citizen was unsurprising: the horrors of World War I, especially the slaughter at Verdun, had devastated the morale of the nation. Some, quite naturally, collaborated: French industry produced goods for the German war effort. But others formed the resistance movement, centered on General de Gaulle and the Free French Government in London. The Maquis and other resistance groups attacked German targets, played an essential part in the

## The most intense areas of fighting

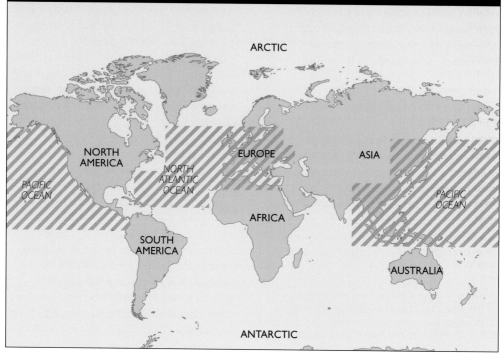

deployment of the Special Operations Executive and of Special Forces, and helped escaped Allied prisoners of war to get back to Britain.

In stark contrast, German society spent the first years of the war relatively untouched by the widespread mobilization of effort seen in Britain. Women, in particular, were not accepted in large numbers for employment due to Hitler's notion that their primary occupation should be the home and childbearing. The Nazi propaganda machine, under the direction of Joseph Goebbels, was very effective in restricting the flow of information to the bulk of the population, about the horrors of the gas chambers and the deteriorating situation facing Germany on the war front after 1943. Economically, Germany was far superior in war production to Britain – even as late as 1944 it manufactured 40,000 aircraft to Britain's 26,500 – but it simply could not match the combined output of the United States and the Soviet Union. Toward the end of the war, some German soldiers were firing wooden bullets because the state had exhausted itself.

In the Mediterranean, Hitler's ally, Italy, managed to survive for almost four years of World War II. Mussolini's gamble in the summer of 1940 brought nothing but failure, hardship, and ultimately, war, to the very

*The Warsaw Rising*
The suppression of the Warsaw Rising is a clear example of the dual threat facing the Polish resistance from east and west. General Blor's underground resistance fighters seized control of the city from the occupying German forces on August 1, 1944, just as the Red Army reached the vicinity of Warsaw. At this point the Soviets inexplicably stopped, allowing the German army to regain control of the city about 10 days later; at the same time, they refused Allied bombers access to Soviet airfields to help the Poles.

mainland of Italy itself. The collapse of the Mussolini regime in July 1943 reflected how the average citizen of Italy was simply unwilling to sustain the ravages and consequences of modern warfare. Mussolini's death at the hands of fellow Italians on April 28, 1945, perhaps summed up the country's general attitude to the war.

The Soviet Union under Joseph Stalin, who matched Hitler in terms of ruthlessness, reeled in June 1941 from the German invasion, Operation Barbarossa – an assault by approximately 4 million military personnel. Life under Communism had always been hard for Soviet citizens, with constant food shortages and chronic

It is widely acknowledged that most civilians in Germany had little knowledge of the disaster about to befall the Sixth Army at Stalingrad. About a month before the surrender, when the situation was hopeless, a young woman wrote to a soldier, "I hope that you'll break the encirclement soon and when you do, you'll be given leave straight away." (IWM HU5173)

economic inefficiency, but now the Nazi threat absorbed all the problems of the past.

World War II was essentially fought and won in the east, with battles of gigantic proportions. The battle for Stalingrad from August 1942 to February 1943 cost the Red Army 1.1 million casualties, of which 485,751 were fatal. The entire German Sixth Army was effectively destroyed in this city, with 91,000 captured, including 22 generals. Soviet ground forces sustained approximately 9 million dead and 18 million wounded during the Second World War. These figures suggest that millions of Soviet citizens went willingly to the fight. This was true in many cases, but for others, the Communist system harshly propelled them into battle often ill-equipped and with no choice. The troops of the NKVD (secret police) summarily shot anyone, no matter what rank, who left their posts.

For the rest of eastern Europe, unluckily sandwiched geographically between two

equally undesirable regimes, the options were either fighting, as Poland and Yugoslavia did, or collaborating with one of the regimes. Poland suffered immensely at the hands of both German and Soviet forces, who massacred thousands of Polish officers, whose bodies were subsequently discovered at Katyn. Yet they managed to resist in cities like Warsaw until they were totally crushed and the city dissolved into civil war. Romania, Hungary, even Italy (whose army was highly unenthusiastic about the venture) provided forces for the Nazi invasion of the Soviet Union, and all would live to regret sending their units into the vastness of the east, which simply swallowed up the invaders.

## The Far East

In the Far East, the rise of Japan was characterized by brutal expansionist policies, in the first instance into Manchuria in 1931, then into China in 1937, French Indo-China in 1941, and Malaya in 1942. Japan sought economic autarky through the creation of the "Greater East Asia Co-Prosperity Sphere," for like Britain, this country suffered from the disadvantages of being an island nation. Its own resources were simply not enough to match the ambitions of the politico-military regime under the overall guidance of the Emperor Hirohito.

Japan's onslaught through China and southeast Asia was marked by brutality of inconceivable proportions inflicted upon the retreating colonial powers. Japanese troops raped and bayoneted their way through the region, treating civilians and captured prisoners in the same ruthless manner. The fall of Singapore on February 15, 1942, in which around 100,000 British, Commonwealth, and local forces surrendered, was the high point of this rapid military conquest. It represented more than just a catastrophe to the European powers in southeast Asia; it was also a signal to Asian nationalists that the yoke of colonialism was not permanent. Henceforth Asia would seek its own way forward.

Japan's Achilles heel in this brilliant military campaign was its shortage of merchant ships: just 6 million tons overall to supply armies in an empire that now stretched for more than 5,000 miles (8,000 km) from north to south. This was a weakness that submarines from the United States would exploit fully in the course of the war.

## The United States of America

For the United States, the bitter shock of the Japanese attack on the US Navy at Pearl Harbor on December 7, 1941, and the subsequent German declaration of war, heralded its inevitable entry into World War II. Roosevelt's pretense of trying to stay neutral while in fact helping the British substantially in terms of warships could now be abandoned as the United States prepared to take on enemies on two separate fronts.

Economically, the war was very good for the United States. The labor force as a whole rose by 10 million to 54 million, of which 4.5 million were women and over 1 million extra jobs were created for black Americans. Population movements were common as industries related to the war effort demanded more manpower: Detroit, for example, increased in size to encompass an extra half a million inhabitants.

The scale of the war effort was reflected in the sheer size of the US forces in the European and Pacific theaters by the end of 1943: 1.8 million military personnel, 17 army divisions, just under 9,000 aircraft, and 515 combat ships in Europe, compared with 1.9 million personnel, 16.5 army and marine divisions, just under 8,000 aircraft, and 713 warships in the Pacific. It was a huge output by any standard, and the posting of Americans overseas brought a generally isolationist population into contact with many other nations and cultures.

Before the large-scale deployment to Britain, US troops were required to watch films that explained the British way of life

### Japanese brutality

The plight of the captured British prisoners of war, especially those involved in constructing the Burma railway, often appears as the dominant image of Japanese brutality. In fact, the siege of Nanking in 1937, in which the Japanese army slaughtered 300,000 citizens, far exceeds those levels of barbarism. In addition, thousands of Korean women were forcibly employed as "comfort girls" for the Japanese troops while on vacation from the front lines.

The loss of Singapore was the worst military disaster for Britain in the entire war. The causes are many, from poor leadership under General Percival through to inadequate defenses (no tanks whatsoever). However, the most important factor was the underestimation of the enemy. Popular notions about the poor efficiency of Japanese troops based on racial stereotypes (one idea held that they were all shortsighted due to narrow eyelids) contributed to the shock when the British and Commonwealth soldiers experienced firsthand the professionalism of the Japanese force. Compounding these facts, the majority of the troops sent into Singapore (when the position was clearly hopeless) were ill-trained and very green conscripts. Several hundred walked off troop ships and straight into captivity. (Topham Picturepoint)

## Total war

and how to adapt to it. Britain was a temporary home to nearly 1.5 million foreign troops during the war, and there were inevitable consequences from having fit young men on the streets with considerably higher wages than their British counterparts. Many American soldiers married British girls – the famous war brides – and took them back to the United States after the war.

The key to Allied success in World War II, due more to geography than to anything else, was shipbuilding capacity. Unlike the Soviet Union, to which Germany was conveniently (uncomfortably at times) connected by land, both Britain and the United States had to travel the oceans before confronting the enemy. Ships and their

The Japanese surprise attack on the US Navy in Pearl Harbor, on the clear Sunday morning of December 7, 1941, was quite devastating to the service and the nation as a whole. Nearly 2,400 US servicemen lost their lives and over 1,000 were wounded. Hundreds of neatly parked aircraft were destroyed on their airstrips, along with seven battleships (sunk or badly damaged) and three destroyers. On paper, it looked like a highly successful strike, but the Japanese missed the most important targets, the aircraft carriers that were away on maneuvers. These ships would more than make up for the disaster at Pearl Harbor with the decisive victory at Midway on June 4-5, 1942, which would signify the strategic decline of the Japanese armed forces in World War II.

precious cargoes were the logistical arteries of war. In Britain, antiquated shipbuilding facilities, working practices, and trade union action (trade union membership in both the United States and Britain rose dramatically in this period) meant that the country simply could not meet the demands of the war. All 39 of the Royal Navy's critical escort carriers had been built in the United States; so too had 99 of its destroyers and virtually all of its landing ships. Britain managed to produce 2.4

*Black American soldiers*
    The US army maintained a policy of segregated regiments throughout World War II, and this was only ended in 1948. Civil rights for black Americans were still a highly sensitive issue in the United States in this period. Just under a million black Americans served in the US Army during World War II, largely in supply and construction units, but one division, the 92nd Infantry Division (Buffalo Soldiers), was heavily involved in the bitter fighting in Italy.

million tons in terms of naval shipbuilding during the war, compared to the United States' 8.2 million tons. With regard to merchant ships the figures are even starker: 8.3 million tons to 50 million tons. These numbers nevertheless represented success in total war; the enemy had been out-produced.

Every aspect of society under such conditions becomes a war-related activity. Britain spent over 80 percent of its GDP on defense during World War II. Surprisingly, out of all the destruction emerged new technologies stimulated by the partnership between academia and the armed forces. The list of new inventions was enormous, from airborne radar called H2S and ASVIII that were essential to the bombing offensive/anti-submarine campaign, to aircraft navigational aids like Oboe. Not least among the innovations was the revolution in conventional weaponry, from aircraft like the Lancaster and B-17 Bombers, to Hedgehog anti-submarine mortars, the V1 bomb/V2 rocket and, at the lowest levels, submachine guns such as the Sten gun. The atomic bomb, of course, was the most devastating new weapon. All of these developments raised the firepower of individuals, units, and formations to significantly higher levels.

Despite the global nature of World War II, some areas were scarcely affected.

Switzerland maintained strict neutrality and in portions of Arabia, Africa, and South America the war cast only a light shadow on daily existence, whereas in certain places, such as Egypt, the consequences of the fighting remain to the present day. Not everybody was forced to fight (in combat) in the name of freedom, and conscientious objectors in Britain worked in agriculture or factories. Some parts of the labor force were simply too valuable to be wasted on battlefields – coal miners, or the "Bevin Boys," named after the formidable Ernest

The most famous of all merchant ships (constructed for specifically wartime use) were the "Liberty" ships, of which over 2,700 were built. Each ship could carry approximately 9,000 tons of cargo and cross the oceans at a top speed of 11 knots. It is estimated that two-thirds of all American cargo shipped abroad during the war was carried on these vessels. The build rate for these ships was incredible due to the revolutionary methods of prefabrication and modular construction that were introduced to the American shipping industry. The SS *Robert E. Peary*, for instance, was built in just four days, 15 hours, and 29 minutes. (Topham Picturepoint)

The V1 flying bomb (commonly called the Doodlebug or Buzz bomb) was a liquid-fueled device with a 2,000 lb (900 kg) warhead and a range of 250 miles (400 km). It was labeled a "terror" weapon because it was imprecise – just aimed and fired to land anywhere on a large target, such as a city. Consequently, civilians in London from June 1943 had the terrifying experience of watching the bombs fly in, hearing their engine cut out, and then seeing them drift downward for a few seconds before detonating. The V2 rocket was also an imprecise weapon, but it gave absolutely no warning before detonation. Unlike the V1, which flew at a height of 3,000–5,000 ft (900–1,500 m), the V2 launched straight up into the atmosphere before coming down directly on its target with a 1-ton payload of explosives. These weapons could not be intercepted and from September 1944 they started to hit London. (Topham Picturepoint)

Bevin, Minister of Labour 1940–45, were one such case.

More and more people turned to religion for guidance during the war, and religion (as it always has) went to war with the troops in the form of combat chaplains and padres on all sides except the Soviet Union, where the state had replaced God. Mass communications enhanced the role of the media in World War II, and newspapers like the British *Picture Post*, journalists such as Walter Cronkite (who became the famous CBS anchorman during the Vietnam War), as well as war photographers like Robert Capa shaped public perceptions in a way that had simply not been possible in the First World War. History was captured in print and on celluloid across the globe, providing an unprecedented social record for the future.

Once the initial German offensive in the west halted on the shoreline of France and failed to knock the Soviet Union out of the war in the east, it became clear that the winner would be decided first and foremost by national output. From those moments onward, military strategies would be determined by the factory worker, the coal miner, the farmer, and the housewife, to name a few. Armies, navies, air forces, and good leadership were still essential to victory, but war on this mass scale required an integrated campaign that linked the home front directly with the front line.

The all-encompassing environment of total war altered the relationship between the citizen and the state. Traditionally wars had been fought at a distance by a chosen few, but this war affected everyone. The survival of the state was in the hands not just of the armed forces but, more importantly, of the people themselves. This

*The atomic bomb*

The development of the atomic bomb under the Manhattan Project was one of the most expensive and top-secret weapons programs in American history. The cost was enormous, approximately $2 billion, and only the president and a handful of military officers and scientists knew about the true nature of the project. The bomb was designed for use against Germany, but it was not ready until after the surrender in Europe, so the target was switched to Japan. On August 6, 1945, the first bomb (Little Boy) was dropped on the city of Hiroshima, killing 80,000 people outright. The second bomb (Fat Man), dropped on Nagasaki three days later, killed between 40,000 and 70,000 people immediately. Including the effects of radiation, both bombs killed approximately 300,000 Japanese citizens over a five-year period.

*Egyptian mines*

There are still millions of British and German mines in the desert areas around El Alamein, near the Mediterranean city of Alexandria, and their exact locations remain unknown. This has a significant local effect on the economy of the region, as local people still suffer casualties and even deaths from these relics.

fact was radically to alter the nature of government in all countries involved in World War II after 1945. It was reflected in foreign policy (the US Marshall Plan giving economic aid to Europe), domestic policy (the welfare state in Britain), new directions (Khrushchev's rise to power in the Soviet Union in the 1950s), and in some countries (such as West Germany and unified Germany today) the utter rejection of war as a legitimate policy direction.

# John Delaney-Nash, merchant mariner

Whether from a neutral or warring nation, the world's merchant fleets found themselves involved in the war from the beginning. No nation could support its war effort with only its own merchant shipping, and even Britain, with the largest fleet in the world, was forced to see a quarter of its vital imports arriving in neutral ships. Subsequently, warring nations could ill afford to let neutral shipping work for the enemy; hence all vessels eventually became targets. The longest-serving merchant marine was that of Britain. The British merchant seaman was going to be at war for six full years, from nine hours after the start of hostilities in Europe, with the sinking of the liner *Athenia*, to the day of the Japanese surrender in the Pacific.

John Delaney-Nash was one such seaman. He survived the six years and saw the war in all of the main theaters of conflict, from the Arctic to the Pacific. But it was to be at a very high price, with some amazing and grueling experiences, not to mention a few near miracles along the way. "I, personally, lost many good friends in the war, and could never understand how I was able to go through it without any harm to myself."

Born in Dublin, in 1910, John Delaney-Nash spent over 50 years in the British merchant marine, becoming a ship's master in 1946. Yet he was not brought up in a seafaring family, for his father spent much of his time in and out of the army from 1888 until the 1920s. Delaney-Nash's first real taste of the sea was at the age of seven when he traveled across the Irish Sea with his family to join his father in Cambridge. There, a couple of years later, he joined the sea scouts. His first job at 16 was working for a tea importer, resulting in many visits to the London Docklands. By the following year, however, he had signed a four-year contract with the Eagle Oil Shipping Company as an apprentice deck cadet, beginning his five-decade career with the sea. Unfortunately, it did not begin auspiciously, as on his first trip his captain killed himself by jumping into the sea.

By World War II, Delaney-Nash had become second officer of an aircraft fuel tanker. His duties in wartime had expanded from those usually associated with second officer, since he was now also the ship's gunnery officer following a course on the Thames River earlier in the year. He was not alone. Royal Navy escort vessels were in short supply and as many merchant ships as possible were being equipped with guns in order to defend themselves against the German surface raiders. In spite of that, the weapons themselves were mostly World War I issue, and it often seemed that their presence was to calm the ship's company as much as to deter the raiders. However, the arming of the ships with one or two weapons was seen as crucial.

By the end of the first year of the war, some 3,400 ships had been armed. Initially the guns were manned by naval reservists and the crews of the merchant ships. Eventually, more than 24,000 Royal Navy personnel, 150,000 merchant seamen, and over 14,000 men of the Maritime Regiment, Royal Artillery were involved in manning the guns of the Defensively Equipped Merchant Ships (DEMS). By the time Delaney-Nash was involved with the Pacific War, he too had large numbers of the gun teams.

*33 DEMS naval ratings under Chief Petty Officer Cooper who had fought the German's great battleship Admiral Graf Spee in the battle of the River Plate in South America. I also had 11 Maritime Ack Ack (anti-aircraft) under Sergeant Minchen, ex-Desert Rats. These men formed the actual defense of our vessel.*

During the war, the British merchant fleet was being asked to supply Britain from all over the world, at immense distances and usually under constant threat from the Germans, and later the Italians and Japanese. The 2,000 miles (3,200 km) or so across the Atlantic were the most dangerous waters for a merchant ship, but the 12,000-mile (19,300 km) journey to Suez via South Africa during the closure of the Mediterranean was no less fraught with danger. Perhaps as worrying for the British authorities was the realization that the merchant marine contained some 2,000 fewer ships than had been available in World War I. True, the ships in service were larger – the average displacement having more than doubled – which enabled far more to be transported, but this also meant far higher losses of material when the ships were sunk.

Even more problematic was the fact that the situation was drastically different from that of World War I. Instead of one major theater of naval operations, Britain by 1942 found itself in numerous global theaters, and at a time when industrial production and wartime demands required feeding beyond anything comparable in the Great War. According to the government statistics, in the Second World War a 500-bomber raid on Germany by four-engine aircraft needed 750,000 gallons (3.4 million liters) of fuel oil, all of which was seaborne.

Delaney-Nash found himself transporting exactly this type of cargo for much of the war, and not just to Britain but also to other operational areas. The losses were high:

*I spent four and a quarter years carrying Aviation Spirit and Motor Gasoline across the Atlantic and saw many ships sunk in my convoys, but I came through without hurt. In one convoy a ship close ahead of us was torpedoed and as she was loaded with a full cargo of some sort of petroleum spirit, swung across our course, exploded in the center and the two halves parted company and went off in opposite directions. My ship, which had no time to avoid the two halves as they blew apart from*

*each other, went straight through the gap and came out of the other side unscathed, even though we were also loaded with Aviation Spirit. The heat from the burning ship was so hot that it scorched our eye lashes and brows and all the hair below our hat bands.*

*We saw members of the crew running around the decks all on fire, some of them jumping into the sea, where they perished in the flaming water.*

Delaney-Nash carried this dangerous cargo across the Atlantic, in the Mexican Gulf and on convoy routes in the Arctic and Indian oceans. However, after four years of war he was beginning to wonder whether he was pushing his luck a little too much.

*I asked our Personnel Clerk Mr. Grabble if he was trying to kill me. In much surprise, he asked what I meant. I told him that I had been carrying clean oil, i.e. petrol and aviation spirit, across the Atlantic Ocean for four and three quarter years in a dangerous war and had he never heard of the old saying about "going once too often to the well?" He immediately got my meaning and said that he would try and appoint me to a nice black oil ship.*

Delaney-Nash got his black oil ship. They were considered to be much safer than his previous aviation fuel tankers. However, on joining his new ship he soon found out that safe was a relative term. The vessel was being prepared as a fleet oiler and supply ship for the new British Pacific Fleet. He would leave Britain in August 1944 and not return until April 1946, spending the time in between supporting warships in the Pacific.

During the war, the losses were tremendous. The merchant shipping sinkings for the Allies after 1942 were in excess of 12 million tons, but continued use of occupied and neutral shipping and massive building programs, particularly in America, enabled the British merchant marine not only to retain its size but actually to grow. Nonetheless, tens of thousands of British merchant seaman were killed during the war. As Dan van der Vat writes about the war on shipping:

*A few vivid images remain: of seamen burning and choking in blazing oil, of sailors instantly freezing to death in the waters of the Arctic, of flashing magazines blowing warships to smithereens, of unspeakably gruesome remains rising from the wreckage of submarines, of aircraft crashing in flames, of the haunting death-throes of stricken ships and of endless cries for help from the water. And here and there a dash of chivalry in a total war.*

Although this comment is written for the Atlantic campaign, it would seem appropriate to use it to describe the war of supply and convoy for all the world's civilian merchant seamen in the Second World War.

Perhaps the only question remaining is: how did people like John Delaney-Nash manage to survive the war and the peace intact and sane? Then again, one of his recollections might give an answer to that:

*Proceeding along E-boat Alley, as it was called, we were attacked by German aircraft. High-velocity bullets were flying all over the place and everyone was busy trying to get a shot at the planes flying through the night sky, when we heard a voice from inside the wheelhouse saying, "Never mind the Germans, Mister, where's the ship ahead?" It was obvious that station keeping was [the] uppermost thing in the Captain's mind. I have always thought that this sort of thinking is very British and what makes the Britisher so strong in adversity.*

# The German fleet is scuttled

The European naval war drew to a close where it had started, in the Baltic. The siege of Leningrad had been lifted by a Soviet offensive that began in January 1944, accompanied by heavy fire support from Soviet battleships, cruisers, destroyers, and gunboats, firing some 24,000 rounds. Increasingly, German naval forces in the Baltic found themselves conducting evacuation operations and fending off Soviet advances that were often accompanied by outflanking amphibious operations.

In January 1945, the Red Army surrounded German forces in East Prussia. This signaled the beginning of the greatest military evacuation ever. Overloaded German ships of all kinds had to negotiate extensive Soviet-laid minefields and run the gauntlet of Soviet submarine patrols. The torpedoing of just three transports, the *Wilhelm Gustloff*, *General Steuben*, and *Goya*, led to the loss of over 15,000 lives. Indeed, out of 1,081 vessels used in these operations, 245 were lost. Nevertheless, during 1944 and 1945, over 2,400,000 people were evacuated to the west in the Baltic.

With the Soviet army in Berlin, on April 30, 1945, Adolf Hitler committed suicide. His nominated successor as Reich President was the now Grand Admiral Dönitz, who established the last Nazi government in the German naval academy at Flensburg-Mürwik. On the evening of May 4, a delegation to Field Marshal Bernard Montgomery's headquarters signed an instrument of surrender to take effect at 8:00 am the next day. This affected "all armed forces in Holland, in north-west Germany ... and in Denmark ... This is to include all naval ships in these areas."

At the end of this war, there was no German fleet to escort to an Allied port. There were submarines at sea and they were ordered to surrender to an Allied port, but many commanders ignored this and either scuttled their boats or sailed them to a neutral port rather than deliver them into Allied hands. On May 7, the unconditional surrender of all German land, sea, and air forces was signed in front of General Eisenhower at his headquarters in Rheims, and it was finally ratified in front of Soviet representatives in Berlin the next day. The war in Europe was over.

# The price of admiralty

The outcome of World War II in Europe had depended on two things: the fate of the Soviet Union and control of the Atlantic. But in many respects the Soviet Union's fate also rested on the sea. Without control of the Atlantic and Arctic oceans, there would have been no lend-lease supplies to Stalin's beleaguered state in 1941 and 1942 and no eventual second front in western Europe. The fact that Nazi Germany was unable to achieve control of the waters around Great Britain meant that a second front was always a possibility. The Kriegsmarine's inability to deny the Atlantic to the Allies made it a certainty.

Germany was eventually reduced by the Allies from all sides, and in the air, on land, and at sea. The hard-won Allied stranglehold

This chart shows the principal causes of damage to Allied merchant shipping. Contrary to the prewar belief of both the German and British naval leaders, the surface ship played only a small role in inflicting damage against Allied merchant ships; the submarine inflicted by far the greatest damage.

in the Mediterranean permitted victory in North Africa, and successful landings in Italy and eventually southern France. The inability of Germany to fend off the maritime power of its adversaries from the coast of northwest Europe meant that the superior resources of the Allies could be applied where wars are ultimately won, on land.

Allied victory at sea came at a heavy price. The Royal Navy alone had suffered 50,860 killed, 14,685 wounded, and 7,401 taken prisoner, a casualty rate of almost a tenth of its wartime strength of 800,000 personnel. The Allied maritime air forces together had lost 1,515 aircraft and had 8,874 of their crews killed, with another 2,601 wounded. In all, 2,714 British merchant ships had been sunk and 30,248 British merchant sailors had lost their lives in the effort to keep the sea-lanes open.

Many other nations had also suffered. For example, in 1940 the Norwegian merchant fleet was, at 4.8 million tons, the fourth largest in the world and included a fifth of the global

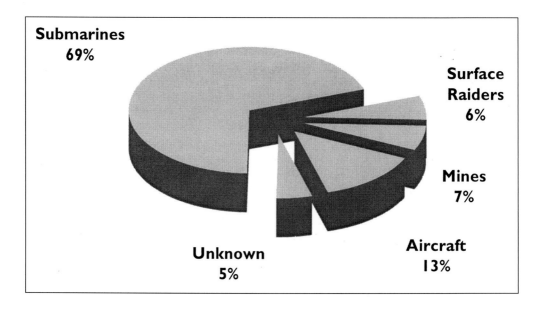

**Submarines 69%**

**Surface Raiders 6%**

**Mines 7%**

**Aircraft 13%**

**Unknown 5%**

tanker fleet. About 85 percent of the fleet, some 1,000 ships, managed to escape German control and served with the Allies. By the spring of 1942 over 40 percent of Great Britain's oil and petrol was being moved by Norwegian tankers. However, more than 500 Norwegian vessels and 3,000 seamen were lost.

Similarly, at the time of the German invasion of Denmark, 230 of its merchant ships with their 6,000 crew were outside home waters and the majority would serve with the Allied merchant navies. By 1945, 60 percent of this fleet had been lost along with some 1,500 Danish seamen. Nearly half of the Dutch fleet of 640 ships was also lost to Axis action, along with some 3,000 Dutch seamen. In all, some 5,100 ships totaling over 22 million tons were lost. The price of admiralty was indeed high.

The price of failure was higher, however, and not just in strategic terms. The German navy had over 48,904 killed and more than 100,256 missing. The navy was destroyed. Of more than 1,160 U-boats, 784 were lost or surrendered to the Allies. A total of 27,491 German submariners lost their lives, which, along with another 5,000 taken

prisoner, represents a casualty rate of 85 percent. This sacrifice resulted in the sinking of 2,828 merchant ships or 14,687,231 tons of merchant shipping, and 158 British or British Commonwealth and 29 United States warships, by far the largest share of the damage wrought by the Kriegsmarine. By the end of the war, 3 million tons of German shipping had been sunk by the Allies, while the Germans had managed to build 337,841 tons, which were supplemented by the shipping they were able to seize in captured ports. About 3,000 German merchant seamen also lost their lives. The navy of Germany's ally, Italy, also suffered heavily: some 15,000 men were killed out of a strength of 33,859, while over 800,000 tons of merchant shipping were sunk.

But it was not just manpower that had to be mobilized and sacrificed. In the long run, the Allies were better able to mobilize their scientists, engineers, and economies. This had been a war of production and technology. The

This chart shows the principal causes of damage to German submarines. The greatest threat to the submarine proved to be the aircraft.

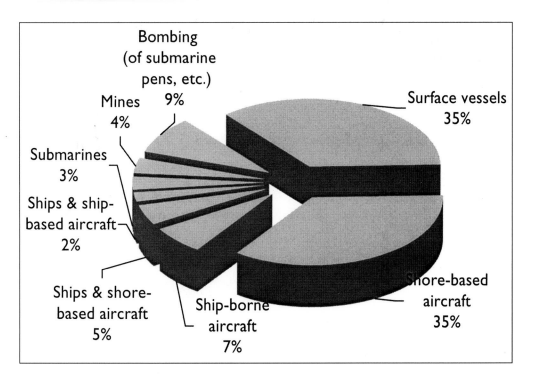

Bombing
(of submarine
pens, etc.)
9%

Surface vessels
35%

Mines
4%

Submarines
3%

Ships & ship-
based aircraft
2%

Ships & shore-
based aircraft
5%

Ship-borne
aircraft
7%

Shore-based
aircraft
35%

conflict proved the danger of the submarine, but it also confirmed the importance of maritime air power in all its guises, whether land-based or operating from carriers. Those who did not heed this lesson were at an enormous disadvantage, as Forbes found off Norway in the spring of 1940, and Cunningham discovered a year later in the desperate battles around Crete. Imagine the difference a completed *Graf Zeppelin*'s air group of Me-109 fighters and Ju-87 dive-bombers would have made to the outcome of the *Bismarck*'s ill-fated foray. However, while the battleship had undoubtedly been eclipsed, the Royal Navy's superiority in this category had certainly prevented the Kriegsmarine's heavy units running amok in the Atlantic. Naval warfare was proved once again to be not only decisive but also complex.

There was also another technical development that, while it did not have an effect on the outcome of the war in Europe, would have a profound effect on the world and, so it appeared at the time, on the immediate future of maritime power. With considerable irony, across the other side of the globe, maritime power made possible, through the amphibious conquest of the Pacific island of Tinian, the construction of an airbase from which Boeing B-29 Superfortresses carrying atomic bombs could reach Japan. With the dropping of atomic bombs on Hiroshima and Nagasaki in August 1945, it seemed that the whole future of traditional maritime power, which had made such a decisive contribution to Allied victory in World War II, was threatened.

# Glossary

**ack-ack** An anti-aircraft gun or anti-aircraft fire.

**amphibious warfare** Military operations that involve the coordinated action of naval and land forces.

**autarky** A policy of national self-sufficiency, economic independence, and nonreliance on imports.

**convoy** A ship or ships accompanied by an escort for protection.

**D-Day** The first day of the Allied invasion of Normandy, June 6, 1944.

**depth charge** An explosive device used against submarines and other underwater targets.

**ethos** The guiding values and beliefs of a specific person, group, or movement.

**expansionism** A nation's policy of territorial or economic expansion.

**fjord** A long, narrow inlet of the sea between steep slopes or cliffs.

**frogmen** Navy divers who do military reconnaissance and destroy underwater obstructions.

**garrison** A military post.

**gunnery** The science of the effective use of guns.

**Kriegsmarine** The German navy during World War II.

**Luftwaffe** The German air force during World War II.

**merchant marine** A nation's commercial ships; the officers and crews of such ships.

**ration** A fixed allowance of food or provisions during a time of war or scarcity.

**salvo** A simultaneous or successive discharge of two or more guns or a rack of bombs or rockets.

**scuttle** To sink a ship by opening or cutting holes in the ship's hull.

**sortie** A military excursion, especially one made from a place surrounded by the enemy.

**Wehrmacht** The armed forces of Germany during World War II.

# For More Information

**Canadian War Museum**
1 Vimy Place
Ottawa, ON K1A 0M8
Canada
(819) 776-8600 (800) 555-5621
Web site: http://www.warmuseum.ca/cwm/home
The museum's permanent exhibition, Forged in Fire, illustrates Canada's role in fighting dictatorships overseas during World War II.

**Imperial War Museum London**
Lambeth Road
London SE1 6HZ
United Kingdom
Web site: http://london.iwm.org.uk
The museum's Second World War galleries document the war on all fronts, including Britain's sea war against Germany and Italy. Exhibits illustrate the threats to supply routes—and the efforts to protect them—in the Atlantic, Mediterranean, and Arctic seas.

**National Naval Aviation Museum**
1750 Radford Blvd., Suite C

Naval Air Station
Pensacola, FL 32508
 (850) 452-3604
Web site:
 http://www.navalaviationmuseum.org
The museum has impressive holdings related
 to World War II carrier aviation, including
 examples of the Corsair, Dauntless, Hellcat,
 Wildcat, Avenger, and Kingfisher aircraft.

**National World War II Memorial**
900 Ohio Drive SW
Washington, DC 20024
(202) 426-6841
Web site: http://www.nps.gov/wwii/
 index.htm
This memorial, part of the National Mall and
 Memorial Parks, honors the 16 million
 who served in the U.S. armed forces
 during World War II and the more than
 400,000 who died. The Web site has a
 link to the World War II Registry listing
 Americans who served in the war.

**The National World War II Museum**
945 Magazine Street
New Orleans, LA 70130
(504) 527-6012
Web site:
 http://www.nationalww2museum.org
The National World War II Museum is

dedicated to the amphibious invasions of
World War II. The museum is located in
New Orleans because it was home to
Higgins Industries, a boat company that
built the landing craft believed to have
won the war for the Allies.

**Naval History & Heritage Command**
Department of the Navy—Naval
 Historical Center
805 Kidder Breese Street SE
Washington Navy Yard
Washington, DC 20374-5060
Web site: http://www.history.navy.mil
The Naval History & Heritage Command
 is the official history program of
 the Department of the Navy and a
 leading authority on U.S. naval
 history. It includes the U.S. Navy
 Museum, a research library, archives,
 an underwater archaeology department,
 and more.

**Web Sites**
Due to the changing nature of Internet links,
Rosen Publishing has developed an online
list of Web sites related to the subject of this
book. This site is updated regularly. Please
use this link to access this list:

http://www.rosenlinks.com/wweh/sea

# For Further Reading

Ambrose, Stephen E. *The Good Fight: How
 World War II Was Won.* New York, NY:
 Atheneum Books for Young Readers, 2001.
Cook, Tim, Sarah Halliwell, and Jim Harkness.
 *The New Grolier Encyclopedia of World War
 II. Volume 4, The Air and Sea War.* Danbury,
 CT: Grolier Educational Corp., 2001.
Crompton, Samuel Willard. *Sinking of the
 Bismarck.* Philadelphia, PA: Chelsea House
 Publishers, 2004.

*History of World War II*, three volumes. New
 York, NY: Marshall Cavendish Corp., 2005.
Hull, Nancy L. *On Rough Seas.* New York, NY:
 Clarion Books, 2008.
Kramer, Ann. *At Sea* (Taking Part in the
 Second World War). London, England:
 Franklin Watts, 2009.
Kurson, Robert. *Shadow Divers: The True
 Adventure of Two Americans Who Risked
 Everything to Solve One of the Last Mysteries*

*of World War II*. New York, NY: Random House, 2004.

Lawson, Robert L., and Barrett Tillman. *U.S. Navy Air Combat: 1939–1946*. Osceola, WI: MBI Pub. Co., 2000.

Monsarrat, Nicholas. *The Cruel Sea*. London, England: Michael Joseph, 2009.

McGowen, Tom. *Carrier War: Aircraft Carriers in World War II* (Military Might). Brookfield, CT: Twenty-First Century Books, 2001.

Panchyk, Richard. *World War II for Kids: A History with 21 Activities*. Chicago, IL: Chicago Review Press, 2002.

Shaw, Antony. *World War II Day by Day*. St. Paul, MN: MBI Pub. Co., 2004.

Shirer, William L. *The Deadly Hunt: The Sinking of the Bismarck*. Updated edition. New York, NY: Sterling Pub., 2006.

Stefof, Rebecca. *Submarines* (Great Inventions). New York, NY: Marshall Cavendish Benchmark, 2007.

Taylor, Theodore. *To Kill the Leopard*. New York, NY: Harcourt Brace, 1993.

Wagner, Margaret E., David M. Kennedy, Linda Barrett Osborne, and Susan Reyburn. *The Library of Congress World War II Companion*. New York, NY: Simon & Schuster, 2007.

Williams, Andrew. *The Battle of the Atlantic: Hitler's Gray Wolves of the Sea and the Allies' Desperate Struggle to Defeat Them*. New York, NY: Basic Books, 2003.

# Bibliography

Auphan, P., and Mordal, J. *The French Navy in World War II*. Annapolis, MD: 1959.

Barnett, C. *Engage the Enemy More Closely: The Royal Navy in the Second World War*. London, 2000.

Bragadin, M. A. *The Italian Navy in World War Two*. US Naval Institute: 1957.

Delaney-Nash, J. *A Varied Childhood and Fifty Years at Sea*. London: 2000.

Ellis, J. *Brute Force: Allied Strategy and Tactics in the Second World War*. London: 1990.

Hough, R. *The Longest Battle*. London: 1986.

Jackson, R. *The German Navy in World War II*. London: 1999.

Love, R. W. *History of the US Navy*. 2 vols. Harrisburg, PA: 1992.

*Merchantmen at War: The Official Story of the Merchant Navy, 1939–1944*. London: 1944.

Muggenthaler, A. K. *German Raiders of World War II*. London: 1978.

Nimitz, C. W., H. H. Adams, and E. B. Potter, *Triumph in the Atlantic: The Naval Struggle Against the Nazis*. NJ: 1960.

Rohwer, J. *War at Sea 1939–1945*. London: 1996.

Roskill, S. W. *The Navy at War, 1939–1945*. London: 1960.

Roskill, S. W. *The War at Sea, 1939–1945*. Volume 1. London: 1954.

Sadkovich, J. J. *The Italian Navy in World War II*. London: 1994.

Sadkovich, J. J. *Re-evaluating Major Naval Combatants of World War II*. CT: 1990.

Terraine, J. *Business in Great Waters: The U-Boat Wars 1916–1945*. London: 1989.

Van der Vat, D. *The Atlantic Campaign: The Great Struggle at Sea 1939–1945*. London: 1988.

Wilson, M. *A Submariners' War: The Indian Ocean 1939–1945*. Gloucestershire: 2000.

Woodburn, K. S. *History of the Second World War: The War Against Japan II*. London: 1958.

# Index

# About the Authors

Professor Robert O'Neill is the series editor of the Essential Histories. His wealth of knowledge and expertise shapes the series content and provides up-to-the-minute research and theory. Born in 1936 an Australian citizen, he served in the Australian army (1955–68) and has held a number of eminent positions in history circles, including the Chichele Professorship of the History of War at All Souls College, University of Oxford, 1987–2001, and the Chairmanship of the Board of the Imperial War Museum and the Council of the International Institute for Strategic Studies, London, England. He is the author of many books, including works on the German army and the Nazi Party, and the Korean and Vietnam wars. Now based in Australia on his retirement from Oxford, he is the Chairman of the Council of the Australian Strategic Policy Institute.

Philip D. Grove joined the Department of Strategic Studies and International Affairs, Britannia Royal Naval College, in 1993 following the completion of two degrees from Aberystwyth in the area of Strategic Studies. He is presently Senior Lecturer in the department and working on a series of articles and a Master of Philosophy thesis concerning naval aviation in the twentieth century.

Mark J. Grove teaches naval and international history in the Department of Strategic Studies and International Affairs, Britannia Royal Naval College, and lectures part-time in the Department of Politics, University of Plymouth. He has a particular interest in amphibious warfare.

Dr. Alastair Finlan teaches in the History Department at the American University in Cairo. Prior to this, he was a Senior Lecturer in the Department of Strategic Studies and International Affairs, Britannia Royal Naval College, of which he is still an Associate Senior Lecturer. He has also lectured at the universities of Keele and Plymouth.